# Joy on the Hills of Life

## *Hope Squires*

*But none of these things move me, neither count I my life dear unto myself, so that I might finish my course with joy, and the ministry, which I have received of the Lord Jesus, to testify to the gospel of the grace of God.* (Acts 20:24, KJV)

I fell in love with running a little more than a decade ago. In those early days, my friend Joy and I ran together at lunch on the hilly corporate campus where we worked. One particular day, we noticed she ran down the hills faster than I could, and I ran faster uphill.

Later that same day, my friend Marchellina stopped by my office.

"I was riding to lunch with a friend and saw you out running. I said, 'Oh, there go Hope and Joy.' My friend said, 'You're kidding, right?'" Marchellina and I shared a good laugh.

Joy and I have spent a lifetime getting used to jokes about our names, and so I sent her a quick email with the co-worker's story. Joy wrote back, "Yep. It was Joy on the downhills and Hope on the uphills." Her words struck me.

It's true in running. We approach downhills with joy and anticipation of a break. Uphills are a different story, and many runners dread the effort ahead. For disciplined runners, "hill workouts" are an integral training component to condition the body to maintain good form and speed through a prolonged run uphill. Running downhill becomes a delightful respite during those workouts.

Isn't the same idea also true for all of us in life? Joy happens naturally when we're living the easy parts of life, the ones that rush by quickly and without much effort. But we struggle to find joy in the harder climbs. That's when hope kicks in. *I hope I can make it to the end of this race. I hope we can get this kid to graduation without strangling her. I hope I can find a better job. I hope we can find a way to keep our home. I hope he can beat this disease.*

While hope and fear often go hand in hand, our story is supposed to be different. Acts 20:24 reminds us to keep hope and joy running together as we each run the unique race God has prepared for us. Even on the uphill parts of our journey, God calls us to be joyful because joy is a great part of our ministry to others who are watching us to see how Christians react in difficult times. Just as runners use hill workouts to become better runners, perhaps we could think of those hard parts of life as our joy workouts, the opportunities we have to practice joy and improve our relationship with God.

When we choose joy instead of more understandable reactions—frustration, anger, sadness, or panic—we offer the world a great gift. We offer a different perspective on the challenges we face in this life. We offer a new way of living through tragic circumstances. We offer a glimpse of the joy promised in heaven. Our joy then becomes our legacy, our ministry, our testament to God's grace.

☙

*Hope Squires published her first book, **The Flourishing Tree**, in 2014, just in time for a move from her native North Carolina to Northern California for her husband's job. If she's not working on her next book or blogging, she's probably outside running, gardening, hiking, or taking photographs. Visit her at* HopeSquires.com

# Joy in the Sky

## *Janet Ann Collins*

One summer evening I was feeling frustrated.

As a widow living far from my kids I had gotten involved in lots of organizations to keep from feeling lonely.

Somehow, running from one activity to another wasn't satisfying, but I knew my life wasn't over yet.

"God," I prayed, "What do you want for me? Is there more service I can do? Should I take on another responsibility in my church? Does someone need help I can give?"

I stepped outside to empty the trash and looked up.

The sky was filled with thin, whips of clouds like I'd never seen before. Although I could hardly feel any breeze, the clouds were moving quickly. Fascinated, I watched them form shapes and patterns, then swiftly move into different designs. In my imagination I could see pictures in those clouds, so I stood and watched them move.

Then, to my amazement, I saw three letters form in a row: J, O, and Y. The word JOY only lasted in the sky for a few seconds, but I realized it was an answer to my prayer.

What God wanted for me was joy.

Nothing I could do would please Him as much as my simple appreciation of His love and all the wonderful gifts He had already given me, like caring friends and the ability to see the beauty around me.

I realized God hadn't become a human being so we would do more good deeds and earn points on a heavenly scoreboard. The Pharisees were already trying to do that.

He came to free us so we can have joy.

❦

*Janet Ann Collins is a grandmother, a retired teacher, and was a foster mother to kids with Special Needs. Her work has been published in many newspapers, periodicals, and anthologies, and she is the author of five books for children. Janet's website is* www.janetanncollins.com.

# CANINE REDEMPTION

## *Jennifer Sienes*

Guilt, shame, and a measure of frustration arrowed its way into my heart with her unwavering, brown-eyed stare. She was judging me, and who could blame her? She spent much of her day in a large kennel, pacing back and forth, waiting for the attention she deserved. A pathetic whine reached my ears— begging wasn't beneath her. It was with the best of intentions that we took in Cheyenne, a German shepherd mix, three years before. But I didn't know then that I'd have to go back to work full-time, and she was now paying the price.

"We *have* to find her a new home," I told my husband, Chris, as we turned our backs on Cheyenne and escaped into the house. "It's not fair that she's locked up all day."

"Have you seen how many dogs need homes?" He led me to his office and, with a couple clicks of the mouse, opened up the California Dog Rescue site with which we'd recently listed her after other avenues had failed. With each page of dog pictures he scrolled through, my heart sank a little deeper.

Someone suggested the animal shelter, but even if we could be assured that she'd find a home, we had no way of knowing if it was the *right* home. And nothing less would do.

*Please, God. Find Cheyenne the perfect home.* This had been my mantra for weeks, but my prayers were colored with shame. Didn't Chris tell me three years ago that it wasn't the right time to get a dog? Did I listen? No. Instead, I regaled him with pictures of Cheyenne as a new puppy until he caved. This situation was a consequence of our sin—mine for not submitting to my husband's decision and his for allowing me to sway him. It was Adam and Eve all over again. *Yes, God, we brought this on ourselves, but it isn't Cheyenne's fault. She shouldn't be punished.*

Chris turned from his computer and gave me a hug. "It'll all work out."

The eternal optimist.

"Sure." I shrugged. If God could raise the dead, He certainly could find a home for one neglected dog. Hadn't He always provided before?

A few weeks later, we were heading out the door, a list of errands in hand, when the phone rang.

"Hello?"

"Hi. My name is Erica. Vicki, from California Dog Rescue, gave me your number. Is Cheyenne still available?"

It wasn't the first time someone had shown interest in Cheyenne. The last person who called wanted to know how Cheyenne would react with chickens (seriously?) and would she stay in an unfenced yard and guard the house. They didn't want a rescue dog, they wanted a highly trained police dog! But

I sensed Erica was different. Could this be the home I'd been praying for?

Erica and her family lived three hours away, but rather than meet in the middle, Chris and I offered to drive Cheyenne to their home. What better way to see how Cheyenne would react—and for us to see where she might be living. My prayer had been for a *perfect* home. Not just *any* home.

The following weekend, we packed up Cheyenne, her crate and a container of her dog food—just in case. If they decided to keep her, we didn't want the transition to be any more difficult on her than possible. We stopped at a park near Erica's house to let Cheyenne out for a while. It was important to Erica that Cheyenne be fairly easy for her daughters to walk. Best to get some of the spunk out of her system before we showed up.

We live in the country, so a "walk" for Cheyenne was letting her loose to run ahead of us. We expected the concept of a leash to be less than appealing, so we were pleasantly surprised when she healed next to us like a pro. She wasn't distracted by children or other dogs. I guess the twelve weeks of dog training she'd had nearly three years before paid off. It wasn't the first time we saw her potential, if only we had enough time to invest.

Erica's house was in a busy town, but much to our relief, it was situated at the end of a quiet cul-de-sac. Cheyenne wasn't used to traffic, so she wasn't what Chris called "car smart." That was the first plus. The second, was Erica herself. A broad smile illuminated her face as she came out to greet us. "We're so excited to meet Cheyenne."

Erica's husband, Ben, wasn't home from work yet, but he was on his way. I knew from our conversation on the phone that

Ben would be the hard sell. However, her daughters, Cordelia, thirteen, and Juliet, ten, were both waiting to see if they had a new member in their family.

They oohed and ahhed over Cheyenne as she dashed from smell to smell in their backyard, her half-mast shepherd ears twitching every time her name was called.

"She's beautiful," Erica said, her eyes taking in the dog like a kid at her first circus. "So many colors."

"Her mother was a very small German shepherd." I stroked Cheyenne's soft ear as she passed by me. "And we believe her dad was a catahoula, which explains her unique coloring." Cheyenne's coat was an odd mix of black, brown and gray. Her thick gray-and-black-striped tail looked like it would be more at home on a raccoon than a dog.

Within minutes, Ben appeared with a welcoming smile and a pocket full of dog treats. It took only moments for Cheyenne to discern who it was she needed to impress. Nobody would accuse her of being stupid. As Ben reached into his pocket, she plopped down in front of him in a perfect sit position, laser focused.

For nearly an hour, we watched as Cheyenne was given a tour of her new home. She sniffed out the rabbit cage and checked out the backyard pond. Then they took her inside and introduced her to each room of the house. She had never been an indoor dog, so I wasn't quite sure what she'd do. But with excitement and curiosity she pranced from the living room to the kitchen to the bedrooms and back again.

"I think she likes it here."

Erica beamed.

Ben retrieved another doggie treat.

Cordelia dropped a kiss on Cheyenne's head.

Juliet smiled shyly from the corner of the living room.

Leaving her behind was harder than I'd imagined. I'd wanted a new home for her—a *perfect* home—and that's what this was. So why was it so hard? It didn't help that as we got ready to leave, Cheyenne attached herself to us, as if she had no intention of being left behind.

"No, no, Cheyenne." Erica took hold of Cheyenne's collar and held her in place.

We passed through the sliding glass door and shut it behind us. I looked back once more—Cheyenne stood there, her black, wet nose pressed to the glass and confusion in her eyes and stance.

"She'll be happy here." Chris took my hand and led me to the truck. "She just needs some time to acclimate."

In the days that followed, Erica sent me update texts along with pictures. Cheyenne with her new collar and bling-bling name tag. Cheyenne being hugged by Juliet. Cheyenne being hugged by Cordelia. Cheyenne and Cordelia, asleep, side by side, on the living room floor. With each text and picture, my heart swelled, and tears stung my nose.

It is because of this joy that I know God hand-chose this family for Cheyenne. I am amazed at how He is so concerned with each and every aspect of our lives, that He'd care where one neglected dog would end up. He blessed us, He blessed Erica's family, and I have no doubt that He blessed Cheyenne, as well.

As Chris and I navigate through the seasons in our life, we will always remember God's faithfulness in even the smallest details. I picture Cheyenne in my mind's eye and my heart leaps. I know she is loved beyond what we could have given her, and she, in turn brings joy to Erica and her sweet family.

*May the God of hope fill you with all joy and peace as you trust in Him, so that you may overflow with hope by the power of the Holy Spirit.* (Romans 15:13 NIV)

*Jennifer Sienes holds a B.A. in psychology and a M.A. in education. After teaching middle school for several years, she was given the opportunity to be a full-time writer. She is represented by Karen Ball of the Steve Laube Literary Agency.*

## RACING WITH MY BROTHER JAKE
### *Abby Drinen*

My brother shades his eyes.

"Is it too bright out here?"

"Yeah," he smiles.

"Want to go home?"

"Not yet."

I sigh. I do.

My mom was waiting for me in the driveway when I got home from football practice tonight. "Take Jake for a walk," she said. So that's what I'm doing. Like he's a dog.

"We can take the shortcut through the park?" I offer.

"That sounds good." He winces and rubs his ear on his shoulder.

"What?"

"Car alarm."

I strain my neck, pushing an ear into the air. A faint bleating echoes in the distance. He's right, but I can't hear it like he does.

"How was school today?" I ask.

"Good. I finished my project for computers."

Jake coded a video game based on a superhero he created, Super Bat. He's a combination of Superman and Batman.

"That's cool. Can I play it, yet?"

"Sure!" His blue eyes widen underneath his dark glasses.

I don't really want to play his game, but I like making him happy. Except when I don't.

"Aw! Yuck." Jake pinches his nose.

A garbage can with peeling green paint stands a few paces in front of us. I smell nothing, not even when we pass by it.

We reach the edge of the park and cut through the grass toward the play structure. A dozen wild, sticky faces dash up and down ramps, glide down slides, and pump their scabby knees on swings. I miss being a kid. Late summer days like this, when your whole world was how fast you could run, or how high you could jump, and the sweet taste of a warm juice box from your mom's purse. The wonders of life before thirteen. Before shaving and girls, after school jobs, and making good grades to get you into the right college.

A woman holds a stick with a circle on the end to her lips and blows. Shimmery bubbles decorate the air, and the little girls around her scream and laugh. Jake tugs on his earlobe.

"You okay?" I ask.

"Yeah, Ben. It's okay. They're just happy."

I smile at one of the girls as a bubble pops on her nose and she dissolves into giggles.

"Are you happy, Jake?"

"Yes," he says, with no further explanation. He probably has more to say on the matter, but the highways in his brain can't always get words to the off-ramp.

Our shoes swish through the grass on the soccer fields. Empty right now, but they'll be full on Saturday. Dotted with red-faced players trying their best to control the ball, and potbellied coaches living vicariously through the team of tiny athletes in their charge.

"Are you happy?" he asks me.

"Mostly. I've got my first test in trigonometry tomorrow and I'm not ready for it."

"But you have Kayla."

"Yeah, she makes me happy." I grin, thinking about how my girlfriend's pretty brown eyes light up when she finds me in the hallway before English class.

"I wish I had a girlfriend." The pout on his lips looks ridiculous for a senior in high school.

"You'll find a nice girl," I say.

"I don't know if I can. Because of my autism."

"Mom says autistic people get married all the time."

"I don't know." He wrinkles his nose.

"What's wrong?"

"Dog poop."

I draw a big breath of air in through my nose. Again, I smell nothing. Jake's like a bloodhound.

On the slope of a hill, we see a couple laying tangled together on a quilt. Two little dogs sleep at their feet. Her golden head is resting in the crook of his shoulder. He's stroking her hair as he holds a book in the other hand and reads aloud to her. His chest starts to bounce, and she covers the giggle on her lips. Must be a funny book.

"I want a girlfriend," Jake repeats and sighs.

"Well, if it's God's will." I say.

"You sound like Dad," he says.

I snort. Never thought anyone would ever say I sound, look, or act anything like my father. I'm the oil to his water, but we're finding our way. We always have sports in common if nothing else. The big smiles and hard high fives we give each other when our favorite team is winning keep us connected. We dive into the greasy nachos mom brings us, and argue about who's the best player or over a call a ref made. Both of us glowing like toxic waste. Game day with my dad is the best.

"Do you think Dad is happy?" I ask.

"I don't know."

That was a stupid question for me to ask him. Jake can't put himself in another person's place. He can't even make guesses about their emotions. He barely understands his own.

"I think Mom and Dad *are* happy," he says.

"Really? How do you know?"

"Well, they talk nice to each other. They don't yell or cry very much." He scratches the uneven stubble on his chin. I need to remind mom to buy him a new razor.

"I guess," I say, thinking about the last argument I heard my parents have. It was over three years ago, and it was about Jake. I was in my room, working on homework. Jake was at occupational therapy. My little sister was at a friend's house.

"I can't keep reliving the day of his diagnosis with you!" my dad shouted. "It was over a decade ago, Anna! The boy's autistic. Accept it and move on."

"But, my baby," my mother wailed. "All his potential, just locked away. But it's in there, Darren. He's in there, and I can't help him get out!"

There was a pause, and then the voices coming from their bedroom got lower. I crept down the hallway and stood at the closed door. Guilt was pushed aside by my curiosity, and I eavesdropped, invading my parent's private conversation.

"You're going to have to find a way to absorb this. A way to deal," he said.

"How do you do it? How do you look at his face, every day, and keep from knotting with pain over who he could have been?" she said between sobs.

"It doesn't matter who he could have been, it matters who he is. And who Jake is, is awesome. I've never met a kid so content. He's okay with his life."

"No he's not! It hurts him when he sees what other kids can do, what Ben can do!" she growled.

I remember feeling a pinch in my stomach at how she said my name. Like I was being accused of being an athlete, a straight A student, a neuro-typical kid. And why didn't she say my sister's name, too? Molly wasn't autistic either.

"I know it hurts him. And yes, Anna, it hurts me sometimes, too. But in those moments, I make a choice. I choose to see all that he has, rather than what he doesn't."

"You choose it?"

"Yes. Jake and I make the effort. And it would do a world of good if you would, too."

"Choose what?"

"To find the joy in being Jake's mom, instead of always stressing over making him different."

I snuck away after that because I heard feet shuffling around and I thought they were about to come out from the bedroom. But my father's words have always stuck with me. I don't always choose to find the joy in being Jake's brother. As a matter of fact, I often resent him. I resent having to play the older brother when I was born the younger. Being forced to take on responsibilities that should have been his. A shameful hatred towards him aches in my gut sometimes. Like when Mom asks me to take him for a walk. He can go for a walk alone. He has a cell phone and has done it before, but she feels better when I go with him. "Just in case," she says.

"Do you think Mom would let us go to Taco Bell for dinner?" he asks.

"No, she probably has something going already."

"Oh. Do you want to walk to Taco Bell with me on Saturday?"

I turn and look up at my hulking brother. Six foot three to my five foot ten. Anger sparks in my chest at his request. I don't want to go. I'd rather spend time with my friends or Kayla. But his toothy grin puts out the flames. I kick my foot behind me and tag him in the seat of his pants. He gives me a playful shove.

"I'll race you to the house," he says.

Racing. Yes, that's something brothers do. Something Jake and I can enjoy together. A lightness rises up from my toes, like I'm in a hot air balloon lifting off.

"Yeah, okay." I angle my elbows and bend my knees. "Ready... set...go!

Abby Drinen likes to write about realistic characters in unreal worlds. Her first novel, **Tenderfoot**, a young adult portal fantasy, is available on Amazon. Abby lives in Northern California with her wildly supportive husband, three stunningly smart children, and red Rottweiler named Paco. Visit her on the web at www.abbydrinenwrites.com.

# THE QUIETNESS OF JOY

## *Sherri Bergmann*

If you were to Google the word "Joy," it appears as a noun meaning a feeling of great pleasure and happiness and as a verb as rejoice.

People tend to view joy as a bubbly, giggly feeling we get when we receive news, such as realizing you're going to have a baby, or a check which came out of nowhere to pay off a few bills, or the job offer you have been waiting for.

However, from the Biblical viewpoint, joy holds a different perspective. Joy is one of the fruit of the Spirit Who dwells inside of us. To think of it as spontaneous occurring during a moment of celebration would be considered incomplete. It is a lasting, deep sense that even happens to us in the midst of our severest trials.

Case in point: Paul, when he was in prison:

*"The crowd joined in the attack against Paul and Silas, and the magistrates ordered them to be stripped and beaten. After they had been severely flogged, they were thrown into prison, and the jailer was commanded to guard them carefully. Upon receiving such orders, he put them in the inner cell and fastened their feet in the*

*stocks. About midnight Paul and Silas were praying and singing hymns to God, and the other prisoners were listening to them."* (Acts 16:22–25)

They were not only flogged, but *severely* flogged. Due to profuse bleeding, each move they made could have exerted excruciating pain throughout their body. Then they were thrown into the inner cell, the most protected and dreadful place to be. Next the jailer fastened their feet with stocks. The meals had to have been less than appetizing.

Yet, what were Paul and Silas doing? They were singing. Singing hymns to God. What? They used what energy they had to sing songs to God. They didn't forsake Him. They didn't curse Him. They sang praises to Him.

And the prisoners listened.

Where did this desire to sing come from sitting in a dank dungeon in pain? Simple. They had joy.

Why? Because the Christ they worshipped was not dead, but real and alive. They had joy because Christ manifested Himself in them. Joy gave the ability to sing even in the darkest times. Because Christ is eternal, the sense of joy is also everlasting.

Paul defied the normal reaction to a situation like being in a dungeon. He kept his joy and faith in the One who also defied what everyone else thought should be—the One who defied death and rose. The joy which comes from knowing in spite of circumstances, Christ will prevail. This truth gave Paul hope and joy as it can for us.

When our loved ones who believe in Him die, we mourn, yet have inner joy knowing where they go, which gives reason to celebrate. They are in Heaven with God in a better place than those remaining. We carry that knowledge and joy. And when time on earth ends, joy will be fulfilled as the moment we've waited for arrives and we see our Creator.

The Christian who rests in the faith of God, in spite of frustration, can have the inner, quiet feeling of joy. Yet this joy shouts because it transcends the world's view of how we as believers should behave. We can choose joy no matter if the stock market crashes. We have peace and confidence in spite of everything going on because we know Who is in control. He bends His ear towards those who trust Him. This brings joy and security.

We don't say, "I'm doomed," and give up when life gets tough. We keep our hope and joy in Christ. We have enduring joy because Christ overcame.

Christ came to overcome death. We who follow Christ can have true joy—even in the midst of trials—because He lives inside of us. Paul and Silas sang in prison, because of joy.

*Sherri lives in Cameron Park, CA with her husband and three dogs. She is a freelance writer and has articles published in local publications, and in previous Inspire anthologies. She credits her Sacramento Inspire Writer's critique group for helping her to become a better writer, and a published author.*

# ON THE OCCASION OF MY 80TH BIRTHDAY
## *Mary Louise Gillis*

You can do an awful lot in eighty years;

You can work and smile and play,

And nearly drown yourself in tears.

I could walk and I could climb,

And read 'til lights were dim.

Could cook and clean somewhat,

But never, ever could I swim.

Saw mountain tops and seas,

Mighty rivers, gracious trees;

Smelled the roses, didn't sneeze.

I was young and pretty then;

Gained some weight, I don't know when.

Well, I guess these days are done.

But though old age is not much fun,

I look up and see the sun.

It's still there, and so am I.

Not quite ready to say, "goodbye."

But, gosh, look here, I'm writing!

*Mary Gillis's head overflows with the enjoyment of words. Her heart beats with new verses. Mary's spirit is keenly aware of ideas from the Lord. Her hands write the poems that burst forth. A feral black cat has found Mary's backdoor stoop, and his daily antics may become new poems.*

# WHEN DOING NOTHING IS DOING MORE

## *Kris Lindsey*

I lifted my empty suitcase to put it back in the closet and noticed my shoulders felt achy and tense. What was up with that? I knew I was stressed when I left for vacation, but after two lazy weeks visiting with friends, meandering through shops, and reclining back and staring for hours at the ocean's horizon, shouldn't I be relaxed? Everything in my life was going well. Why were my shoulders still tense?

On closer evaluation, my whole body was tight and achy: my chest, my hips, my feet. *Enough is enough. If I don't calm down I'm going to make myself sick.* I vowed to dig in and make a conscious effort to relax my muscles throughout the day, then realized this sounded like a New Year's resolution. And how long do those work? Hmm.

About that time, I happened to read a familiar Bible passage in John 15 about Jesus being the vine and us Christians being the branches. It says that if we stay connected to Jesus, we'll bear much fruit. Then the last part of verse 5 jumped out at me: "Apart from me you can do nothing."

That line always irritated me. Of course I could do some things apart from Jesus. I could do a whole range of things, from tying my shoe to completing complex tasks. What did it mean when it said I could do *nothing?*

Then it occurred to me, this verse was talking about bearing fruit, and the fruit of the Spirit includes peace and joy. How was I doing at producing *that* on my own? My tense muscles told the story.

*Okay God, this time I'm getting serious about letting You steer every detail of my life.*

As an experiment, I decided to try taking this verse—that I could do *nothing* without God—literally for a while and see what happened. So I asked God to help me brush my teeth. I asked God what I should eat for breakfast and which tasks I should do next. Before I left to go out the door, I'd ask Jesus, "Am I forgetting anything?" And sometimes I'd suddenly remember an item I needed to take with me.

Whenever I put Jesus in the lead, I felt my shoulders relax and my posture straighten up. My attitude also improved. Instead of trudging forward with my head down, I felt like I was hanging with my best buddy.

But when I forgot about God and went about my plans on my own, I found myself making mistakes. I forgot to take my medical records to my new doctor's appointment. I went to another office on the day it was closed. I mixed up facts in conversations and had to be corrected. It seems I couldn't do as many things on my own as I thought, and at the end of the day I felt drained and frustrated.

I always thought of myself as a competent person. I worked hard to figure things out. That is who I am—a thinker. So taking the stance that I could do nothing without Jesus was hard for me. But I began to see that treading through my day without Jesus was like walking in the dark with a small flashlight. I could do it, but I'd only see a fraction of the picture and be prone to stumble. Doing things with God was like traveling in style in the light.

In the process of doing this exercise, I discovered I put a lot of responsibility and high expectations on myself—in both performance and relationships—and this responsibility weighed me down. But when I said, "Okay God, You're in charge," the weight of responsibility lifted. The knot in my stomach loosened. The dark force that kept me from moving forward disappeared and the room brightened. Suddenly I felt hopeful, because with God all sorts of good things are possible.

Over the next few months, whenever I said, "I can do nothing without Jesus," it felt like I was on a tandem bike with God in the front, steering and pedaling, while I sat on the back seat enjoying the ride. This new way of doing things taught me how to let go and rely on God.

With God in the lead, my job was to listen. Since I started this exercise, I've been doing a lot more listening. "Jesus, what do You want me to do next—this, or that, or something else?"

Sometimes God answered by giving me an impression—either all clear to go, or a negative feeling to stop and do something else. Sometimes, if I was really listening, a new idea outside my main line of thinking gently popped into my head. Not an order. Not required. But I knew to take it seriously because it was probably God's best for me.

After I received direction, my job was to do what I felt God was leading me to do, still listening and asking for His help. Because, "I can do nothing without Jesus."

Of course, I knew I *could* do things on my own, but why would I want to? My lightened heart and quenched anxiety were good enough reasons to put God in the lead. But on top of that, the optimism and surge of energy I got made me feel like I was really living.

The apostle Paul said, *When I am weak, then I am strong.* (2 Corinthians 12:10). By taking the attitude "I can do nothing without Jesus," I'm finally learning how to *Be strong in the Lord and in his mighty power* (Ephesians 6:10, emphasis added). The more I rely on Jesus, the more His power, peace, and joy flows into me.

Previously published on Kris's website.

🐝

*The desire of Kris's heart is to grow closer and closer to Jesus, and to help others do the same. She enjoys discipling new Christians, and spending time with family and friends. Read more about her journey to find greater peace and healing at www.krislindsey.com.*

## THE SHADOW OF JOY
### *Susan Sage*

Put the cape on...

No, the dress.

Don't forget the right shoes.

You won't fit in without the right shoes.

How do I act as I enter the room?

Shall I smile? Should I be serious?

Do I just listen?

Or can I speak?

When will I find a place

To truly be myself?

Where someone will like me,

If I am my true self?

Will I ever get to be me,

Or must I always dance this dance?

It's too costly to be real.

Someone might get hurt.

Me.

Then from inside…deep inside,

I seem to remember.

God loves me, just for me,

And doesn't care what I wear.


If that's true, and oh, how I hope it is,

Who does He expect me to be?

I read somewhere He'd love me still

Even if I didn't dance perfectly.

I know He loves everyone

But, could that include me

Even without the right shoes?

What a thought.

Wait, what's this I feel?

Could this possibly be?

To be loved no matter how I look or what I do?

I think I'll stay here in the shadow of joy.

*Susan Sage loves the adventure of writing. She writes Bible studies, devotionals, poems, dabbles in fiction, and is currently in re-writes for her first non-fiction book. Susan also speaks to women's groups whether teas, retreats, luncheons or wherever God gives the opportunity. Her passion is encouraging women in their walk with God no matter where His sovereign plan takes them. Currently, she is focusing that encouragement to those who live with chronic illness and pain. You can find her at susansage.com, @SusanMSage, on Facebook, Google+, and Pinterest where she posts her weekly blog.*

# RIDING IN THE FRONT SEAT

## Rosemary E. Johnson

The fair is so big. Janine trots beside me, purse swinging from her elbow, sunlight winking off her glasses, mouth open in wonder.

I just want to go home.

But she isn't about to stop. It's our last day together, and she's determined to have fun. Janine is the brave one. Janine is the fun sister. My idea of fun is sitting in my armchair, listening to Bach and knitting for my grandchildren, with my cat stretched across my shoulders. Janine says that's for fuddy-duddies who have no sense of adventure.

Well, this old fuddy-duddy has no sense of adventure.

I adjust my hat to block the sun from my eyes. Sweat trickles down my neck and dampens my dress. My knees ache. I've been walking too much today. Janine agrees to look at the exhibits, but she drags me through the displays of flowers and quilts so fast that I don't have time to admire much at all. She slows down some when we go through the children's exhibits and giggles at all their cute creations.

In front of a papier-mâché donkey, she turns to me, eyes round with a terrifying sparkle. Wisps of hair float about her face, and a smile tugs at her cheeks. "Let's go on a ride."

"Are you kidding me?" I clutch my purse to my chest. "We should have lunch and go home."

Janine clucks her tongue. "Now Lorraine, you know I'm not going to leave this place until I get you on a ride. What about the Ferris wheel?"

My head spins and my stomach churns at the thought of going higher than any building in Nevada County. "No. Positively not."

Janine pushes her glasses up the bridge of her nose, still smiling. "We'll walk through them and choose one." She's determined, and I know I can't stop her.

I pray she gets her thrill from walking through the racket and the speeding contraptions. We wind through lines of chattering young people. The aroma of popcorn and cotton candy hangs too thickly in the air, and the screams from the haunted mansion do nothing to comfort my nerves.

Nearby, children laugh on the merry-go-round. The music on the carousel is bright, cheery, and off-key. It doesn't go fast. But it does go round and round, and watching more than a few moments makes my head spin. No, thank you.

Janine pokes my shoulder. "I want the one with the black mane."

I shake my head. "No, let's find a different ride."

She looks at me from the side of her eye. "All righty then. But I would've enjoyed getting acquainted with that lovely mare." She glances beyond the merry-go-round and gets that look again.

My heart sinks.

"Lorraine." She grabs my hand and points wildly. "We're going on that one."

I follow her gaze to a new-fangled roller coaster, looping and twisting on a skinny wooden track. I feel my eyebrows rise right into my hairline and hug my purse tighter. The handles dig into my chest. Why can't I think of an excuse?

"Come on, sissy." Still gripping my hand, Janine gives me a yank.

I stumble after her, captured, wishing I could melt into the ground. If only I'd agreed to the merry-go-round!

The line is long. Good. Perhaps I can weasel my way out of it before we reach the front. I find my handkerchief and dab at my forehead. Now that I'm nervous, it feels like I'm standing under a spigot. The roller coaster zings around the tracks, up and down like a crazy thing.

I already feel sick. "I'm too old for this."

"*Pfft.*" Janine rolls her eyes behind her spectacles. "Just because you're a grandma doesn't mean you can't go on a roller coaster."

"My grandchildren want to see me again." My pleas aren't working.

Janine tilts her head, smiling. "Don't worry. You're not going to die."

We're suddenly on the platform, watching the youngsters ahead of us pile into the cars. I squeeze my purse handles, hoping we won't make it onto the ride this time.

I hope wrong.

The ticket man doffs his hat when Janine gives him our tickets. She climbs into the cushioned wood cart and pats the space beside her. My knees go weak. Of all the seats we could've gotten, we have the very front one. I will surely die.

I look over my shoulder, but the line of people is growing, and they're pressing me forward. Too late to back out now. I plop down beside Janine and fan myself with my hand.

She nudges me in the ribs, cackling. "This is going to be fun."

I doubt that.

She laughs and wiggles, jostling my side while the ride fills up. I keep my eyes forward, watching the man running the controls. How can he look so bored? His hand is on the lever. He pushes it down...lower...lower...and we lurch forward.

At first it's slow as the ride cranks up. Chains rattle somewhere beneath my feet. Janine flashes me a grin and waggles her eyebrows. I press my feet onto the floor and grip the side of the cart with one hand, pushing my purse into my lap with the other.

Faster and faster we go, bobbing up and down. Wind rushes into my face. My hair blows back, tugging on my hatpins. My pearl necklace bounces against my throat. As we pick up speed, I let go of the side and reach up to hold my hat down. Beside me, Janine hollers and whoops.

Our skirts suddenly fling up in our faces. Janine shrieks with joy. I grab at the fabric, trying to force it down, but it flaps in my face, puffing out in front of me. Oh, if the minister's wife could see me now! I laugh and look over at Janine. Her head's thrown back, mouth open with laughter, and if any more air fills her skirt, she'll rise up and float clean away.

Faster and faster we go. It's like we're flying on the tire swing above Grandpa's pond, years ago. Nothing is holding me back. I let out a whoop, and my heart soars in pure happiness. This is the best idea Janine's ever had.

The ride slows, and our skirts settle back down. Janine thrusts up an arm and cheers as we grind to a halt. I sit there and laugh until my side hurts and the ride attendant has to motion me away.

My legs are a little wobbly when I get out, but I'm busy wiping the tears from my cheeks. I'm still breathless with the fun of it. Every time I look at my sister, we both giggle like we're little girls again.

Janine touches my arm as we make our way down the stairs and onto the grass. "Let's eat lunch and go home."

"Are you kidding me?" I grin. "Let's go again."

*Rosemary E. Johnson lives in the Sierra Nevada Foothills with her parents and her cat. She is currently working on the first book in an epic fantasy series. When she isn't writing, Rosemary enjoys reading, learning languages, playing piano and violin, and painting. You can visit her website at* www.rosemaryejohnson.com.

# I Wish You Joy

## *Tessa Bertoldi*

I would give to you Joy—

The quality of life to be alone with self.

Quietly turning thoughts inward to meditate on direction.

To know who you are and where you are going.

That certain peace of mind that comes from knowing self, direction and escaping manipulation.

To be still and know who God is and to seek His will as your own,

To wait for Him.

I wish you Joy.

*Tessa Bertoldi is a Technical Writer, translating Engineer into English. She is a staff volunteer for NaNoWriMo, SF Writers Conference, and Writing for Change. Tessa's current projects include a Sci-Fi novel and educational guide to fill the gaps for her adult foster children. Her website is* https://tessabertoldi.wordpress.com

# Reserved Joy

## *Michelle Janene*

Teaching called to me, even as a young child. But I am an introvert. I don't mean I'm a little introverted. No. On all the personality tests I've taken, I score 90-98 percent introvert. As a teacher, I spend my days with sixth graders. Sixty or more students come through my door each day. Parents stop by and send email, and, of course, I work with a great staff. Introverts aren't shy or anti-social. They get their energy from time alone. Therefore spending eight hours a day with upwards of seventy people can be extremely exhausting. But God has blessed me with this job.

The rest of my life, I'm a writer. Good position for an introvert—well, until it comes to actually talking to people. As an indie author, all those contacts, events, and launches fall to me to organize. And it means talking to people. I feel a panic attack coming on. I can't even sign a book with someone standing there waiting. I misspell my message, run words off the edge so I have to hyphenate them in weird places. I can't think and it becomes a real mess.

But being overwhelmingly introverted is not my only oddity. I am also a phlegmatic. In general, phlegmatics are pretty even people. We don't like to get too excited, or too angry, or too depressed, or too excited, or too—you get the picture—no extremes. I have been told, "Fake a little excitement," when people give me something or do something for me. Even that can be a little hard. I never want to be "wild and crazy."

Okay, I'll admit it. I'm weird. I don't quite fit the mold—for anything I do.

So, as I said, I have a few quirks. How does an extremely introverted phlegmatic express the joy of Christ? Dictionary. com says joy means "the emotion of *great delight* or happiness caused by something exceptionally good or satisfying; keen pleasure; *elation*." The Bible talks about loud celebrations of great joy with instruments and dancing. Miriam and the women danced and played tambourines when the people crossed the Red Sea (Exodus 15:20). David danced before the Lord when the ark came to Jerusalem (2 Samuel 6:14).

*And on that day they offered great sacrifices, rejoicing because God had given them great joy. The women and children also rejoiced. The sound of rejoicing in Jerusalem could be heard far away.* (Nehemiah. 12:43)

And Psalm 149:3 tells us: *Let them praise his name with dancing and make music to him with timbrel and harp.*

Dancing, singing, elation, noise that can be heard far way—I think I'm getting hives. But can there be such a thing as reserved joy? Calm joy? I believe so.

*The precepts of the LORD are right, giving joy to the heart. The commands of the LORD are radiant, giving light to the eyes.* (Psalm 19:8)

I do have the joy of my salvation, and I do love to sing hymns and choruses—alone in the car and quietly in the congregation. Even an introverted phlegmatic can have eyes shining with the new life of Christ within them.

The blessings of God overflow in my life. God is forever good, and worthy of worship. I love praising His name and teaching my students of His amazing love for them. There is no greater joy for me than filling pages of fiction with the truth that brings joy to us all. My heart flutters, my breath catches. The excitement in this knowledge dances over my skin and keeps a smile on my lips.

My joy may not be dancing in the streets, loud, or even noticeable. But the joy of the Lord is my strength. And I experience it every day.

*Michelle Janene lives in Northern California, though most days she blissfully exists in the medieval creations of her mind. She is a devoted teacher, a dysfunctional housekeeper, and a dedicated writer. Michelle published* **Mission: Mistaken Identity** *in 2015 and has both contributed to and helped to edit the Inspire Anthologies.* www.TurretWriting.com

# TEACH A MAN TO FISH

## *Alan Dixon*

*"You thrill me, LORD, with all you have done for me! I sing for joy because of what you have done" (Psalm 92:4 NLT)*

I packed up my truck and decided I would try fishing in a place I'd often driven past during my frequent commute. I figured one day I'd stop and try my luck at this fishing hole. I considered taking my fishing pole with me one day and casting my line out a few times during my lunch break. My wife urged me to do it, but of course I was always far too busy to do such a dastardly task. I finally made the time and so away I went. The only drawback to my fishing excursion on this particular day was that there were 20-30 mph wind gusts.

High winds and catching fish don't normally go hand-in-hand. I sat in my chair all day long, catching nothing. Every time I stood up to check my bait or to stretch, the wind blew my chair over, even after I propped rocks up against it to hold it in place. I spent more time chasing my chair than fishing. After waiting so long to try this fishing hole, I thought I could at least catch one fish. The wind and the odds were against me.

As I often do when sitting in nature and admiring God's majesty, I prayed. "Lord, You know my heart. If there is any way I can catch just one fish today, please make it possible. I know the winds are bad, and I haven't caught anything all day. If You find it in Your will to bless me today, please make it happen." Within minutes, I felt a bump on my pole, then a tug, next a pull. I set the hook by pulling back sharply on my fishing pole.

Thrilled, I reeled in a hearty, striped bass that day. I actually caught two fish, but one was too small to keep. What great joy God brought into my life with such a small act of His kindness.

God heard my prayer and answered it, not because of anything I did, but because He chose to bless me that day. The Lord thrills me daily, not just by allowing me to catch fish, but by all He does in every aspect of my life.

*Lord God, thank You for Your majesty and ongoing willingness to bless us each day. Help us continue to look to You in all areas of our lives and praise You as You thrill us by Your actions. In Jesus name I pray, Amen!*

*Dr. W. Alan Dixon, Sr. recently completed his doctoral degree in organizational leadership. He is currently the Regional Sales Director for General Nutrition Centers and is working on developing leadership programs, publishing both articles and devotions to encourage new leaders.*

# DON'T BYPASS JOY, MY LOVE
## *Erin Bambery*

This is not my ideal Valentine's Day. *It's definitely about a heart, but who knew my fiancé would need a triple bypass?* Both of his parents had cardiac disease. We were relieved by the news he did not have a heart attack and no damage was detected.

It's pre-op day. As we enter the hospital doors, my battle with fatigue and fear increases. I draw a deep breath, and squeeze David's hand.

He kisses the top of my head. "God promised me, 'I will take the stony heart out of you and give you a heart of flesh.' I didn't realize He meant it literally."

We sit and wait for room registration at 6:00 a.m.

*Father God, bring David through surgery and be his powerful healer.*

They call us in for David's room assignment and give us his co-pay amount. *We owe how much? Maybe if I blink my eyes rapidly, the numbers will rearrange into a better formation.*

Nurse Brian interrupts our shock and ushers us into the blue-curtained prep area. He instructs David, "Change into this wrap-around blue gown, open at the back, with lovely ties."

*Um, where do I go while he changes his clothes?* My engagement ring doesn't mean David and I are *that* familiar.

Loud beeps startle us and alert staff to a Code Blue. *Blue curtain, blue gown, Code Blue–might as well add my spirits to the blue list.*

A woman's monotone voice drones through the intercom and echoes into the hall, "Dr. Stevens, STAT, Cardiac Intensive Care Unit."

Next, a tranquil male voice drifts through the intercom, "Good morning, time for prayer." The prayer floats overhead, woven with powerful words like, "Help the suffering, healing, wisdom."

David looks up in tears and closes his eyes. "Unexpected serendipity."

Within four hours, all the pre-op is complete and we're eager for the comforts of home. *I NEED big chunks of chocolate. Truffles, no, a chocolate heart!*

❧

The clock points to a little over two hours since his surgery began. *Breathe. Pray.* I am in the family waiting room, sitting directly across from the gray, metal surgery doors. *Maybe someone will update me soon.*

*Father God, I believe You kept him from death and want to give him more life. I must juggle so much. Be my amazing manager! This mountain of events is crushing me—impossible unless I yoke myself to Your strength. I can't do this alone. You can do it! I MUST trust the outcome of Your perfect timing.*

I open my iPhone and tackle the mountainous "to do" list:

• Call the leasing agent for David's apartment. *Is the new apartment ready to move in?*

• Schedule appointment for Mom to see her new apartment. *Mom's spirit is low. Remove her fears. Help her adjust to a new neighborhood and give her the joy of an adventure.*

• Call both of Mom's doctors. *Why are her meds lost in transit to the pharmacy?*

• Tax documents to the preparer. *Hope I set all those papers aside when I packed my files.*

• Call my real estate agent. *My home appraisal came in $2,000 under the selling price. The buyers and their lender will need to battle it out. I don't have time to worry about that. God, please take care of that dispute.*

• Call Salvation Army. *Pick up boxes of donations. Make sure my sister's boxes aren't mixed into the pile.*

• Call Sis. *Did her husband finish the sheetrock and flooring? God, grant him favor with the inspectors, schedules, and approvals. We need You to manage their home building project. You know she needs to move out before my escrow closes.*

• Schedule junk haulers. *Remember to give them the sheet metal pieces from my roof repair.*

• Email sitters for David's 24-hour care. Enough for several weeks, when he is discharged. *If that happens in the midst of moving, I need to cover ten morning and evening shifts.*

• Email our wedding minister regarding his plane reservations and arrival time. *I need to select the rehearsal date and time.*

• Email the florist and photographer with selections. *Some of my other wedding plans can wait for a month or so, but I need Your help with those details, too.*

A voice scatters my thoughts. "Hi, how are you doing?"

I look up from my list—David's family stands before me.

One of his brothers asks, "Any news yet?"

"I haven't heard. Surgery is estimated at four to six hours. It's been about three."

Twenty minutes later, I recognize David's surgeon when he strides through the swinging metal doors. Beads of sweat drip from under his cap, down his face, and into his mask beneath his chin.

I jump from my chair and step towards him. *What's wrong?*

In a low tone, he confirms his reputation as the quickest surgeon, "We are finished. Surgery went well. I am happy with the results. You can see him in about two hours."

Right on time, we enter David's recovery room. We stare at the heated air mattress lying on top of him. He is pale, still on a respirator, and tubes trail out. *Good thing they warned us about what he would look like. Go home—four days until moving day.* Innumerable boxes await my attention.

ↄ

Two days post-surgery, David develops an irregular heartbeat.

I greet him with a kiss on his pale cheek.

He puffs, "I have A-fib. My heart beats hard. Like a symphony in my chest—terrible—all night long. Dr. Levi wants an echocardiogram. Possible shock—blood thinners. Something's wrong. Honey, can you call the nurse?"

*Breathe.*

Nurse Hannah informs us, "Any minute the echocardiogram will be done. If he needs the defibrillator, we will slightly sedate him."

I text our people and request prayer for the A-fib—some of them had healthcare careers. A few explain that a defibrillating machine used on a *conscious* person is very painful. They described it like a jump start.

*No! I don't like this at all.*

The petite technician enters with the echo machine. She speaks in soft, broken English, "I see only this heart is dry."

Nurse Hannah responds, "Dry?"

"Yes. I see only that."

Dr. Levi arrives. He discusses the results with the petite technician and Nurse Hannah. He orders concentrated IV fluids.

Twenty minutes pass. Dr. Levi states, "No sinus rhythm for sixteen hours, still A-fib." He sends for the defibrillator team.

*I can't watch!* Thoughts flee, like an erased script, and leave a blank page in my mind.

"You really don't want to be here for this." Tension is behind a team member's smile. She assembles the machine with speed and shoos us out of the room.

I wander down the hallway with David's brother. My thoughts return. I want to get out of earshot, because someone told me they scream from the pain. *Breathe. Is David's brother afraid? Keep silent. I can't cry with his brother watching me. PRAY. What can I ask? Father God, David says You PROMISED him a new heart. Would You give him a defective one? That's all I can think. Scripture says You give perfect gifts. Please fix his heart so they don't have to.*

*Breathe,* I tell myself.

Five minutes pass. I call the ICU desk and ask for re-admittance.

A nurse answers. I hear—several voices, a big commotion, and laughter—*a party?* She blurts out, "Sorry, come on in."

The buzzer sounds and the doors swing open.

We approach the nurse's station on our way to David's room.

*I don't see any balloons.* Dr. Levi and the defibrillator team are the noisy ones. I stop and stare. They are before a computer screen, pointing, and making exuberant, garbled comments. He calls out to me, "We didn't have to do it! I was just about to use the defibrillator and he went into sinus rhythm. It fixed itself!"

One team member declares, "I literally had the paddles, primed and ready, just about to place them, and it switched rhythm! We couldn't believe it! We are so relieved!"

They bob around Dr. Levi and laugh.

I must give Him credit, "Thank God! *He* fixed it!"

A few of the team nod and smile—some turn away. One credits the intravenous fluids.

*But I know, God. You fixed David's heart rhythm and delivered him from horrible pain. We relied on highly skilled staff and medication, but the A-fib persisted. "The heart is dry," sounded strange, but they listened and gave David fluids. Our loved ones prayed, and You answered. You did the part only You can do—fix a struggling heart. My fears are gone.*

My heart erupts with joy!

❦

*An Inspire Writers member, Erin Bambery wrote "Meaghan O'Meara's Bowl," published in the 2015 **Inspire Forgiveness** anthology. Erin lived abroad and traveled extensively. Her artwork includes over one hundred murals, plus illustrating the successful first edition of **Little Known Tales in California History**. Erin enjoys her grandchildren and being a newlywed.*

# THE MEANING OF JOY

## *(A Haiku)*

### *Analiese Bondar*

How to describe joy.

Your heart leaps towards the moon.

Hope compels your soul.

*Analiese attends a Christian middle school in Northern California. In her free time Analiese loves reading, listening to music, and dancing. She wants to be an animator when she grows up. Her hobbies include drawing, writing, running, swimming, and spending time with her family.*

# Joy in the Unexpected
## *Sandra Trezise-Heaton*

Africa. From pyramids to apartheid is a vast, mysterious continent—violent, bloody, breathtakingly beautiful, once the seat of an advanced civilization. It is a continent where bondage and poverty are often a way of life.

I traveled to Africa many times, fascinated by its ancient history and antiquities, towering monuments, the boundless wealth of the pharaohs, and an advanced society that thrived hundreds of years before western culture existed.

My fondest memories are of the animals. Magnificent does not begin to describe them as they are free to roam and interact in their natural habitat unburdened by cages and artificial surroundings.

At night, I sat on the veranda of our compound and watched animals arrive at their watering hole. They had an apparent arrangement with each other about the order of their appearance. I often wondered if they were performing some grand dance. Each group of animals strolled, drank, and bathed in the shifting light from the sun setting at its most flattering angle. Even the great predator lion came to the water peacefully. The hunt and kill would take place elsewhere, not in front of the tourists, or where the precious water was needed by all—more civilized than much of the human race.

One of my favorite memories is of the night my roommates and I were headed to bed. A strange sound filled the room, a whooshing exhalation of sorts. We were told the curtains must remain closed at night to prevent attracting animals, but our curiosity got the better of us. We snapped off the light and parted the panels.

There, with its enormous head pressed close to the window was a magnificent elephant. Its ears flapped rhythmically. Nostrils expanded and contracted as its trunk inspected the glass. It must have been a juvenile, because its body fit perfectly within the area of the window glass. He stared at us. We stared at him. We were, in a sense, taking the measure of one another without fear or malice.

I held my breath and marveled at his size, touched by the sacredness of connection between man and beast—a profound moment.

He soon tired of the two-legged creatures in the glass cage. He turned and walked away, huge rump swaying, small tail swishing from side to side with the plodding motion of his enormous legs. The ground shook slightly with each step. He disappeared into the darkness.

We did not move or speak for some time.

*Sandra writes creative non-fiction. She is published in the **Inspire Promise** and **Inspire Victory** anthologies and in many caregiver publications. She writes about her care giving experiences with her mother, her travels, and her late-in-life marriage.*

# THE BEAUTY OF GOD'S JOY
## *Judith Rose*

Oh God—the beauty of Your Joy!

Shimmering with raindrops, the leaves of Your trees

dance to the breeze of Your touch.

Folded flowers, having risen too early,

wish they had stayed abed.

And berries, bright in red slickers,

laugh at Your showers, like birds in the sprinklers.

It is joyous, Lord, Your mirth and humor,

It is wondrous, Lord, the beauty of Your Joy!

❦

*Having to retire early from nursing, teaching, and water coloring due to a long list of chronic illnesses and spine problems, Judith has thoroughly enjoyed writing poems, prayers and essays, but mostly devotionals.*

# THE TRUTH

## *Madison Wright*

A cloud of misery and heartache shadowed me daily just like Olaf in the movie Frozen. Moving from my hometown was a joyless endeavor. The long car ride with my baby brother and opera music proved to be added torture. A fall down the stairs, a broken ankle, and crutches added to my misery.

How could my life get any worse?

Ten minutes late the first day of school, hobbling on crutches, I found my classroom. One quick breath and I walked into the classroom. It was like I stood in the woods at night all alone with millions of eyes watching my every move. I slunk to the teacher's desk. I just wanted to go to my old house, hide under my blankets, and never come out again.

The teacher made me stand and introduce myself in front of the whole class. The worst thirty seconds of my life so far.

I thought things were getting better at lunch when a group of girls, led by a girl named Ariana, came up to me and brought me to their table. They told me to sit there every day. They seemed nice. The rest of the day continued to be bearable.

Over the next few days I started to change my mind about the girls who first befriended me during lunch. The next Monday, I saw one of the girls snatch someone's homework off their desk and rip it into shreds without being noticed. I hoped it was a one-time thing and she wasn't really like that, but then I noticed more evidence these girls weren't very nice. One girl put graffiti on another person's locker. Another even locked someone in a locker.

By now I started to realize one girl in particular was the cruelest of them all. Ariana. She had been disrespectful to the teachers. Behind the math teacher's back Ariana said, "I'd throw a party for whoever shot her out of a cannon." She stuck gum on the walls and in the carpets, requiring hours to remove.

But she wasn't only rude to the teachers, her fellow classmates suffered too. Ariana restarted people's computers losing their work. She punched, tripped, and stuffed them in trashcans. She stole their lunches, and wrote notes telling them they should kill themselves, and put them in their lockers. The only people spared were her friends and I.

By the end of the first week I was considering breaking our friendship. I had gotten home earlier than the rest of my family and I was standing in the kitchen eating a Popsicle when I heard voices outside my window. It was Ariana. "Don't ever try to talk to me about Jesus, or I will take this matter to the principal. Why would I want to be a Christian anyway, to make me a loser like you? No way!" she said.

I felt like a knife had stabbed me in the heart. It hurt me to see Arianna saying those words to the girls I had admired from afar. Amidst all of the torment this group of girls remained calm. I would have exploded under similar pressure.

I wondered what helped them remain so serene.

I sat down with a piece of paper and my lucky pink pen and wrote a note:

> Dear Christian girls,
>
> I heard what "my friend" Ariana said to you today. It really hurt me. Your actions show me that your heart is fully devoted to your God. I don't understand how you were so calm when Ariana was bullying you. If it isn't too much to ask, could we meet somewhere during lunch or after school tomorrow to talk about Christianity?
>
> Thank you, Addison

The next morning, I quietly slipped the note in one of the Christian girl's lockers. I really hoped this was the right locker, or I could get in so much trouble. We are not supposed to talk about religion at school.

I saw them during my next class and gave them a quick smile. They answered with confused stares, but returned my smile. I didn't understand how Ariana could be so mean to such nice girls.

I followed the girls to their lockers and sighed in relief when one of them stopped at the locker where I had inserted the note. When she opened the locker the note tumbled out and she stooped to pick it up. As she read the note I saw her face light up and she quickly shoved it into her friend's hands.

Once her friend finished reading, they looked at each other with huge smiles on their faces.

"We should meet her in the lunchroom," said the girl with the note still in her hands.

I stepped out of my hiding place and said, "Perfect, I'll see you guys there." With that I skipped off to my next class.

I looked around the lunchroom trying to figure out where the girls were sitting.

"What are you looking for?" a nasty voice snarled behind me. "We're over here—like always."

"Oh, nothing," I quickly replied.

Ariana didn't seem too convinced but shrugged her shoulders and walked of to join her friends.

I saw the Christian girls sitting in a corner of the room and when they saw me their faces lit up. I ran over to meet them. "Hey guys, I baked you some cookies last night," I said as I pulled out a box from my lunch bag.

"Really? Thank you," they replied as they ate the cookies.

"What are your names again, I heard Ariana talk about you guys, but I didn't pay attention to your names," I said.

"My name's Taylor, and this is my friend Alexis."

"Nice to meet you guys, my name is Addison, but I'm sure you knew that already."

"We're so glad you wanted to talk. We'd love to share with you," said Taylor. She handed me a Bible opened to a book in John. She pointed to a verse, *For God so loved the world that he gave his one and only son, that whoever believes in him shall not perish but have eternal life.* (John 3:16). "God died for us and if we accept His gift we are saved and can live with Him forever in heaven," Alexis said.

Over the next few days they gave me lots of verses to read and they always explained them to me. Even though we'd only met, it was like I had known them all my life. Things were peaceful with them around. After six days of Bible reading, I made my decision. I wanted to accept God's gift and live with Him in heaven forever.

When I told Taylor and Alexis they rejoiced in my decision. They told me to repeat this prayer after them: "Dear Heavenly Father, thank You for dying for me so I could be saved. Please forgive me for all that I have done wrong. I will continue spreading Your Word and will read the Bible daily so I may know more about You. Please help me to follow You for the rest of my life. Amen."

I am so glad I had made that decision. I continue to read the Bible everyday and I tell others about Jesus. I even told Ariana about Christ, and she accepted His gift too! Ariana and I became friends again.

My new friends brought such joy to my life, but not as much joy as the Lord gave me.

The Lord works in amazing ways. You might not think your current situation will help you, but God knows what is best for you and He can make something great out of a bad situation, even moving far away from home.

God wants to use you to do amazing things, all you have to do is say yes.

❦

*Madison is a middle school student in Northern California. She loves to read, digesting one or two books a week when school doesn't get in the way. She hopes to be a teacher when she graduates. For now she enjoys hanging out with her friends.*

# FULLNESS OF JOY

## *Ellen Cardwell*

During the 1960s and '70s, miraculous things happened to ordinary people. I was one of those people.

While holding hands in a prayer circle, I felt a warm sensation on my forehead, near my hairline. Before I could react, the heat moved down my head toward my mouth, and I burst out laughing. Not polite, socially-acceptable laughter. Belly laughter, hearty and loud. And long.

This could not have happened in our polite denominational church. The spiritual climate there had diminished as our new pastor preached a social gospel at the expense of evangelism. For weeks at a time he didn't mention the name of Jesus. Many of us hungered for God and sought fellowship with like-minded believers in small groups. That's how I happened to be in one.

That particular night, we listened to a tape by the author of *Prison to Praise*. The idea that we could praise God in all things because He would work everything for good was brand new to me. It was as if there was a vacant slot in my interior into which this truth fit perfectly. It meant that there was no cause for regret, worry, or fear. This was how I could obey our Lord's command to be anxious for nothing. And that's why I was so full of joy, to the point of overflowing.

My temperament is primarily melancholy. If there's something wrong, I can find it. If it's not wrong, I can imagine it. In the natural, I am an Eeyore. But because of God's Spirit, I am a happy Eeyore, a cheerful Charlie Brown—or should I say Charlene? God brought balance to my life through the Word and His joy. I'm constantly grateful He saw my need and filled it.

God gives us a taste of His joy in the present, and that taste makes us hungry for more. Our hunger *will* be satisfied, because there's so much more of it ahead of us! Psalm 16:11 declares that *in your presence there is fullness of joy* (ESV). Thank you, Lord, for the times we experience joy now, and for the anticipation of an eternity in Your presence when we will all know the fullness of joy.

*Ellen Cardwell writes inspirational non-fiction pieces, and articles for the general public as well. She has been published in **The Upper Room**, Inspire anthologies, **El Dorado Hills Telegraph, Senior Times**, and **Around Here** magazine. Her first book is a work in progress.*

# Joy Comes in the Morning
## *Loretta Sinclair*

*The pain of childbirth is not remembered. It is the child that's remembered.* ~ Freeman Dyson

The night you were born was both the most joyful and the most agonizing of my life. At least I thought so, until the day you disappeared.

At 4:00 pm I was getting ready to leave work. Another long day with not a minute to myself. All I wanted to do was get home and relax. My phone rang. Private caller. Probably some salesman. I answered anyway.

"Hi, Lori? Chris's mom?"

"Yes."

"This is his employer." What's going on? They've never called me before. "Do you know where he is?"

Panic. My vision went blurry and my palms began to sweat. "He left at 4:30 this morning to go to work." Almost 12 hours ago.

"I don't want to alarm you, but he never made it."

Too late. Alarm bells were in full-blown panic alert mode.

"Don't worry, we have people out looking for him."

*Don't worry.* My stomach wrenched and I wanted to vomit. Waves of hysteria beat at my brain. This was worse than labor. This was life and death, and he was missing.

I ran to my boss. "I have to leave."

"Try not to worry. He's probably okay."

Probably? That didn't comfort me.

My coworkers chimed in. "I'm sure everything's fine. He's probably with some girl."

"He's not with a girl." He's more responsible than I am. We never miss work. Why was everyone just trying to make me feel better?

I called my ex-husband. "Chris is missing," was all I could get out. In shock, he said nothing. I hung up.

My phone rang again. His employer. "Do you know the route he usually takes to work?"

To work. "Yes." My mind raced. I could barely get the words out. "Normally he would take the freeway, but today since he was starting at a new fire station, he took a shortcut through the Mendocino National Forest." Stop, and breathe. "He said there would be no cell phone reception there."

"Right. That's good information. Let me check some things." Click.

The next eight hours were a blur of one phone call after another. Sheriffs' departments in three counties, Missing Persons reports in three counties, employers in two counties (he works two jobs at two different fire districts), California Highway Patrol in three counties, a rescue helicopter, and Search and Rescue in two counties all calling to get as much information as they could obtain. And then family.

I called my mom first. We have not always been as close as a mother and daughter should be, but in a crisis she will drop everything and come running. That she did. Immediately getting on the phone and notifying the entire family and being the liaison so I could focus, she held us all together during the crisis.

My sister was the first person at my house. We have fought like cats and dogs our entire lives. We are oil and vinegar together most of the time, but she was there before I got off the phone with the first of the search teams. The oldest of my brothers, also a fire fighter, got involved in the search, taking his own vehicle and family up to join in the search. My youngest brother (our last sibling) who was out of town at the time, led the prayer warrior charge. He and my sister-in-law notified everyone they could, and got everyone talking to God for us.

11:30 pm my phone rang for the last time that day.

"Lori?" It's Sean, Chris's boss. We've had to call off the search due to darkness. We'll start up again at first light."

"It's supposed to snow tonight."

"Yes." The depression in his voice was clear. "We know. We're doing everything we can. We have every available person possible out there, and every agency at our disposal. Try not to worry."

Try not to worry? He has no clue what he was saying. The only thing that could save Chris now was a miracle.

"God. I know You're there. You promised never to leave me. You took care of us both the day he was born, and I am begging Y5ou to take care of us both now."

That's when the real pain set in. I tried to sleep, but awoke about every twenty minutes all night long. Just like labor, my gut wrenched, I couldn't breathe, my head ached. Both nights blurred together, though thirty-two years apart. I would pray while I was awake, and then doze from sheer exhaustion. When I awoke again I would still be praying.

Will he be healthy? Alive? When can I hold him? Again?

Will he have ten fingers and toes? Still?

Is he hungry? Cold? Can I really do this?

And then the real question. The one that made time stand still, and sent shivers of fear down my spine. What if the outcome is not what I want? Life isn't about me and what makes me happy. Sometimes God's will for me is different from what I would choose. Would I still follow God?

"Father, even if I have to bury him, I will not turn from You, or Your will for my life." That came at 2:53 am, both nights. The exact moment that he was born, and the exact moment that I gave him back to God.

At 5:45 am the phone rang. Panic seized my heart again. I grabbed the phone from my chest and hit ANSWER.

"Lori, it's Sean. Just letting you know the helicopter is on the pad and warming up. They will launch the rescue again as soon as the sun peeks over the horizon. Search and Rescue ground teams are also gathered and ready to start." There was a long pause. "We're going to find him today." There was a confidence in his voice that was not there the day before. I continued to get updates around 9:00, 10:00, and 11:00. Nothing new to report. Still searching.

Then…

12:00 noon. I was at the gas station filling up my car. Nothing was working. I was tired of the empty phone calls and assurances that everyone was doing everything they could. I was going to go up myself and bring my baby home. The phone rang one final time. "Lori, we found him. Search and Rescue is on their way right now to get him. As soon as he's safe in the car I will let you know. Initial reports show he is uninjured."

I couldn't speak. If I had not been sitting in my car I would have fallen to my knees. All of the emotion, anger, fear, and pain fell away, and I felt the assurance of God.

*This is my will. He will come home to you.*

All that I could say was "Thank You," and it stupidly came out of my mouth over and over again until my wits came back. I think it was enough. Complete peace and calm washed over my troubled heart.

I felt God smile.

∽

"*For I know the plans I have for you,*" *declares the Lord,* "*plans to prosper you and not to harm you, plans to give you hope and a future.*" ~ Jeremiah 29:11

*Author, entrepreneur, consultant, Medical Billing Specialist, mom, and lover of God, Lori lives in Northern California with her two kids, three dogs, and cat Princess. She works full time by day and dreams of fantasy worlds by night. Her website is* www.SinclairInkSpot.com

## CHRISTMAS IS THE TIME WE CELEBRATE
### *Betty Overstreet*

Christmas is the time we celebrate our Savior's birth

When he left his home in Heaven to live here on earth

He was just a newborn babe, no room at the inn

Destined to give His life, to save us all from sin.

An angel of the Lord appeared on earth that night

Speaking to the shepherds, filling them with fright

"Do not be afraid, I bring you news filled with joy

For tonight in the city of David, is born a tiny baby boy"

*Suddenly there was with the angel a multitude of the heavenly host*

*praising God and saying, "Glory to God in the highest,*

*and on earth, peace, good-will toward men."* [1]

The wise men from the east were in awe of the sight

When they saw the Christ Child's star, shining so bright

They traveled along, searching night and day

Bringing gifts for the babe, lying in a manger filled with hay

I love the story of how they all traveled far

The shepherds from the fields, wise men following a star

To worship the Christ Child, and shower Him with love

Praise God our Father for sending His Son from above

*Betty Overstreet began writing for God several years ago. She has created six books and always has another in the works. Her first endeavors were poetry. She learned that every song begins with a poem. She is now a Christian country songwriter.*

[1] Luke 20:13–14 (KJV)

# THE OIL OF JOY

## *Beth Cantrell*

Tears streamed down my face into my ears. Seeing through bleary eyes, I swung my hand in the general direction of the bedside table. When I made contact, the tissue box went sailing across the bed. I grabbed and pulled out several tissues, smothered my eyes, and sopped my tears.

*Why? Why? Why did he die?* I flopped down on the pillow, and my blubbering wave became an uncontrolled storm.

*Why? He was well and active. His mind was clear. He was full of the zest for life, eager to explore each new day. He usually arose out of bed with a praise song and prayer.*

Rolled over on my side, I patted the bed where he lay the previous night. The sheets were cold; there wasn't a warm body to snuggle, no deep breathing that turned into soft snoring.

The tears gushed up from deep down in my middle. I shook and thrashed around on the blanket. After a time, I stretched and lay spread eagle, calmed by exhaustion.

*Knock, knock.*

*That has to be my son.* In a flurry, I sat up and banged my feet on the floor, smashed down my hair with my palms, and made the effort to turn up the corners of my mouth.

He opened the door. "What are you doing in bed? It's time to have breakfast and read the Bible." His eyes were red, his mouth quivered.

Groping for the tissues, I didn't make a connection, instead I snuffed and wiped my face with a corner of a pillow case. Choking down a sob, I said, "I'll be right with you, just let me wash."

❦

Six months passed, and my fifty-five-year old son, Paul, continued to wake me every morning. "Mom, get up, get dressed, and come read the Scriptures. If Dad were here, he would want you to still be faithful to the Word."

I'd had another sleepless night, and only started to doze in the last hour. In my stupor my legs slid over the side of the bed. I made an off-balance effort to stand, but fell backward on the sheets. I again rose up, but slower, shrugged on a robe, scrunched into slippers, and shuffled to the breakfast table.

Paul strode around the table, pulled out a chair for me, and then took his place. "The first reading today is in the Old Testament."

Blinking my eyes to squeeze out the night, I opened my Bible at the bookmark.

Paul pointed to Psalm 45. "Here it is, Mom, right where we stopped before."

"My Bible says Forty-five was one of the nine royal Psalms. It addressed the king of Israel and showed Christ as King."

"This time, you start first." He wiped his eyes and blew his nose. "I see by the markings in his Bible that Dad read the forty-fifth Psalm many times over."

Through misty eyes I read. At verse seven I stopped and reread it:

*You love righteousness and hate wickedness; therefore God, your God, has set you above your companions by anointing you with the oil of joy.* (Psalm 45:7)

"Mom, keep going. Oil is used in healing."

"I think we are to call on His name for guidance to love right doings and hate wicked doings. If we do that, God sets us apart. He anoints us, as He did Jesus, by the Holy Spirit's oil of joy."

"Good job, Mom. Then we are blessed."

I lowered my head to drink in the message. "I need to ponder those verses."

"Do it later. We must move on or I'll be late to catch my bus for work." Paul flipped to his bookmark in the New Testament. "We are at Jude. It's only one page."

"The introduction reads that for its size, Jude probably packs the greatest faith-wallop in the New Testament." I slowly read and savored the words.

When I finished, Paul read the page. "I like the part at the end."

"Pastors say those words to the people when church is over. Read verse twenty-four again."

Paul read, "To him who is able to keep you from stumbling and to present you before his glorious presence without fault and with great joy."

I smiled. "Jesus does that for us."

Paul rose from his chair, bent over, and kissed me on the cheek. "I'd like some of that great joy. I'll take it with me and pass it around with my smile." He gave an enormous belly laugh. "When I get home from work, I want to find you dressed and cooking dinner using that joy oil."

"Have a God day!" I called after him.

"You, too." He nodded and closed the front door.

Paul had grown far past the abilities our pediatrician predicted. True, his lack of breathing when he was born caused some brain injury, but now he was a grown man caring for me. *I must snap out of this gloomy frame of mind and start living fully.* I pushed my chair out and stood, determined not to go back to sleep, but to get busy.

Dressed, I made my bed. With the table cleared and the dishes rinsed and in the dishwasher, I picked up the newspaper and looked at the smiling child on the front page. Her happiness at finding her kitty stirred the same response in me. While I sang, I gave a *whisk* and a promise to the floor with the broom.

After sanitizing my hands, I poured the coconut oil into the crock-pot to brown the roast and placed vegetables on top to cook for supper. Satisfied the house was halfway in order, I sat in my easy chair.

*Come Holy Spirit. Show me how to rise above. Other widows, after fifty years of marriage, have bounced back to again seek God's work. Why don't I?*

The Bible on my lap fell open to a well-read passage. On Sunday afternoons my husband and I used to read whole books of the Bible together, aloud. As a widow I had gotten away from that practice. Once again it was time to treasure the Word.

At chapter one of Ruth, I mused that I was a widow like those three women, but more like Orpah, who retreated when her husband died. I saw clearly the need to be faithful as Ruth had been. Was I finally ready to leave the old country of bereavement? In this new country was I ready to follow, and be under God's covering—to be used by Him? Reading the four chapters out loud, I saw my necessity to abandon my last six months and cling to God, the lover of my soul.

I slipped to my knees in front of the chair. *Oh, God, I exchange this self-focused apathy to gain Your energy for listening and serving. I want to follow Ruth's example. I want to grow through this grief. My joy comes as You prepare me for Your purpose—to bring me a meaning-filled life out of death.*

God's mercy would stop this lethargy that I'd brought on myself, and kick off the force of darkness. The pain of the cross looked forward to the joy of victory. I wouldn't waste this pain, but now I'd focus on God and grow into fullness of service.

*I put my life anew in Your hands. Birth in me a new joy to share Your comfort with others. Trust me to help new widows, and to keep moving forward in encouraging others to become unstuck.*

I took my bottle of Aloe Vera oil and lavished my arms and shins. After turning on a CD, I closed my eyes and let the music and the oil soak in and uplift my body's praise.

☙

When Paul walked in the front door at ten after five, I was singing. He turned toward the kitchen and took a deep sniff of the onion and meat aromas. "Well you must have had a wonderful day with Jesus. The way you always did. I'm glad you're back to being my mom, anointed by the oil of joy."

*Beth Cantrell shares personal experiences writing fiction, devotionals, legacy, and poetry. She leads the Vacaville Inspire Writers and is Secretary for the Inspire Board. Beth lives with her new husband and her special-needs son.*

# FINDING JOY WHEN IT SEEMS IMPOSSIBLE
## *Chrissy Drzewiecki*

God surrounds us, daily, with gifts of joy. And there is joy to be found in the people we come in contact with, the places we visit, circumstances we find ourselves in, and in the things God blesses us with. But, sometimes, in order to receive joy, we need to be still.

In Psalm 46:10 (ESV), God tells us, "Be still, and know that I *am* God." (emphasis added)

What does that mean? To me it means: Stop! Stop the Overs— over-thinking, over-analyzing, over-doing, and over-feeling. Just, be, still. Seriously. Halt—right now—whatever you are doing that may be causing loss of joy, and ask yourself a few questions.

• Are the thoughts I'm allowing my mind to dwell on clouding my eyes from seeing Jesus—from seeing Him clearly?

• Is what I'm spending my time doing just busywork? Or is it truly significant, following what Jesus wants me to be doing at the moment?

• Is what I'm feeling from God? Or is it the evil one demanding attention and turning me away from the joy God has for me?

If you don't want to spend time over-thinking, over-feeling, or over-doing—choose instead to "Stop Over" to God's place, and be still.

Where might that be, you ask? Everywhere. God is everywhere, in control of everything, aware of your every thought. You must be willing to stop and be still.

My life has been filled to overflowing with seasons of immense and intense sorrow including the loss of both my parents, my only brother, my best friend, my mother-in-law, and so many others. Was there joy during those times? Yes, and no. Yes, in the knowledge they were on the shores of Heaven with Jesus. And no, I could no longer hear their voices or visit with them. However, at each new rising of the sun, Jesus filled my heart with joy in the form of memories shared together with those I lost.

Decades ago, as a single mom with two boys both with extreme personality differences, there were many days I experienced no joy—only frustration, bitterness, anxiety, fear, and a feeling of complete inadequacy. The frustration and bitterness I felt was due, in part, to their absent father choosing not to give time to them or be a part of their lives. The fear was because each day was a challenge, and I did not know if I would have enough resources for our next meal. The anxiety was because of the boys' constant sibling rivalry and anger as they acted out their own frustrations, hurt, and confusion. And the overwhelming feelings of inadequacy were because I wasn't convinced I was cut out to be their mother. I was the sole provider of all things in parenting these two gifts from God, two beautiful beings, and I felt helpless.

Soon, joy came. Little by little, it grew and I became a proud mom. I had joy when watching my oldest play baseball, celebrated joy when they learned to ride bikes, experienced joy when witnessing my youngest act in his first play at church. And I had an indescribable joy when they gave the smallest gesture of love in the form of a hug or a "Thank you, Mom."

I taught them to respect women, to hold open any door with a gentleman's attitude of, "Ladies first." I taught them to help carry heavy items such as groceries and to take the trash out. I found joy when *they* found *their* passions. One chose sports, and the other chose acting. Now it warms my heart to see what wonderful fathers and husbands they are. I find joy in that I played a role.

And, oh what joy I had when the first grandchild was born. I thought my heart would burst with love when I looked into her beautiful, perfect face. And now, the Lord has given me four wonderful grandchildren.

Now, my joy is found and shared with my husband—my best friend—of nearly 24 years. After 17 years, I'm retired from a stressful job at a tech company and embracing the not-so-busy lifestyle.

I write this, in my most joyful place. It is the wonderful, glorious swing on my patio. It's here, sitting amongst my flowers, watching my hummers and butterflies flitter from one feeder or flower to another and listening to the finches and doves sing their songs. My heart explodes with life's simple, joyous pleasures.

Throughout all the seasons of my life, I've learned to find joy in the smallest things and how to be still. To see, hear, feel and touch the hand of God in my life. This is the only joy. Our Heavenly Father gives it to those who call upon His name, and He gives it unconditionally and abundantly. We just need to learn how to receive it.

Where will you find joy today—right here, right now? Choose to "Stop Over" to God's Place—I promise you will be blessed.

Trust me, just, be, still.

*Be still and know that I am God.* (Psalm 46:10, ESV)

*Chrissy Drzewiecki loves the Word of God and writing about Him. In 2011, her story "Money Dog—Her Weight in Gold" was published in* **The Dog Next Door by Revel Books**. *Chrissy's stories can also be found in* **Inspire Faith, Inspire Promises, Inspire Forgiveness,** *and* **Inspire Victory.** *She also has poems in* **Inspire Glimpses of God's Presence.** *She is currently writing a mystery/romance trilogy. Visit her at* 4giggle.com.

# PICTURES OF JOY

## *Xochitl E. Dixon*

Denise Tipton rolled over on her side, tucked the comforter under her chin, and prayed she could forget every moment she'd experienced over the past three days. She squeezed her eyes tighter when she heard the soft thuds of little bare feet padding across the hardwood floor in the hallway. Five light taps on her bedroom door bashed against her temple. *How am I supposed to face my little girl today, Lord?* She winced as the door creaked open, remembering the nasty thoughts rolling through her head every time she'd nagged Evan about greasing the hinges.

Ellie's voice flittered into the empty room. "Are you going to wake up today, Mama?"

Silence choked Denise.

*It's not Ellie's fault her daddy's not coming home. Be my strength, Lord. For her.* She exhaled as the door clicked closed. Counting the slow steps, she knew Ellie had made it to the pantry. Alone, again. Being a big girl, while her mom barricaded herself in her bedroom and fell apart.

Clinking dishes and muffled laughter from the television mocked Denise's hollow heart. Would she ever laugh like she used to? She pulled the covers over her head, breathing in the fading scent of her husband's musky cologne. She'd told Evan she hated the red comforter since the day he'd brought it home. Home? Two people. Three bedrooms. *How can this home feel so empty, Lord? There are still two Tiptons left.*

Denise pressed her nose into the crimson comforter and inhaled deeply. She didn't want to forget that smell. Evan's smell. Could she get away with wrapping the king-sized cloth around her neck like a cape? She huffed and frowned. Heroes wore capes. Ellie's distant giggles proved the only brave Tiptons had names that started with the letter E.

Tossing the bedding aside, Denise sat up and pressed her back against the oak headboard. She pulled her knees to her chest and glanced at Evan's tattered, leather-bound Bible that now rested on her nightstand. Why couldn't she remember the verses they'd memorized? Why couldn't she walk by the faith that had brought them together?

Her cheeks warmed as the sunlight poured in from the window. How would she ever regain the trust she'd lost in the God who allowed them to be torn apart? *Will I ever feel joy again, Lord? Or even be the mom I used to be?*

Closing her eyes, Denise tightened the hug around her shins. Evan had admired her long legs since the day they'd met, the first day of their senior year in high school. She'd raced home and told her mom that she'd spend the rest of her life looking into Evan Tipton's chocolate brown eyes. Yet, there she sat alone, twelve years later. *Please. For Ellie. Help me, Jesus.*

Denise hid her face in the crumpled sleeves of Evan's dress shirt, just one of the shirts that doubled as her pajamas ever since the Navy chaplain knocked on their front door. Had it really only been three days since she'd lost her best friend?

Fast thuds from the hallway jerked Denise into action. She swiped at her dampened cheeks, hopped out of bed, and almost made it to the bathroom before Ellie burst through the door.

The two Tiptons stood at attention, barefooted and facing each other. Both dressed in jammies way too big for their petite frames.

Denise squinted, trying to slow her breathing as Ellie struggled to hide a large piece of poster board behind her back. Disney princesses smiled as they paraded lies on the front of the little girl's ruffle-sleeved nightgown. Why did she let Evan make her believe in Happily Ever After?

Deep dimples kissed Ellie's cheeks. "I'm glad you're done napping, Mama."

Tugging at her too-long sleeves with trembling fingers, Denise shifted from one foot to another. "I see you made a peanut butter and jelly sandwich."

Ellie nodded, wild wisps of raven curls framing her face. A few swirly strands stuck to the hints of breakfast on her chin. Her tongue swished back and forth across her sticky upper lip like windshield wipers on high speed.

Denise couldn't look away from those large brown eyes. Evan's eyes. An unexpected smile pinched her with guilt. *How can I be happy at a time like this?* She shielded her chest with her arms.

The attempt to protect the remnants of her heart failed as her little girl closed the gap between them.

The two Tiptons stood toe-to-toe.

Ellie cleared her throat and gazed up at her mother. "I've been making something special for Daddy's Home-Going Celebration."

Funeral. Why hadn't they taught her to say funeral? Denise balled her hands into fists.

Bringing the poster board from behind her back, Ellie steadied it with outstretched arms. "I finished this morning."

With clenched teeth, Denise stared at the family pictures that covered every inch of the paper canvas.

"Let's look, Mama." Grabbing her mother's wrist, Ellie giggled. "You'll love it." She pulled Denise toward the rumpled bed where three Tiptons once cuddled and laughed and fell asleep together during thunderstorms. Sprawling across the bed on her tummy, Ellie placed the collage in front of her. She tapped the space next to her with an open palm. "Sit with me." She rested her chin on crossed arms and stared at the pictures. Bending her legs at the knees, she twisted her ankles inward and clapped the soles of her bare feet together.

Denise's chuckle ushered in a soft snort that thrust the two Tiptons into a fit of snickers.

Ellie sat up and pointed to a picture glued to the top right corner of the board. "Daddy taught me how to clap with my feet. See?"

"I know."

"You took that picture of us."

Climbing into the bed next to her daughter, Denise said, "I remember that day."

"He had the best smile ever. Didn't he?"

Denise gently untangled one of Ellie's wild curls. "You have that same smile."

"I know." Ellie caressed a photo of her Daddy's face with her fingertips. "I miss him."

"Me, too." Denise rubbed her daughter's back with one hand. "Me, too." She tapped a snapshot taken of the three Tiptons at the beach. "That was a good day."

Ellie leaned against her mother's thigh. "We had lots of good days with Daddy."

Denise scanned the memories displayed before her. "Lots." Her gaze stopped on a burst of color. She used her ring finger to trace the edge of a lime green Post-it Note taped to the center of the board. "What's this?"

"My hope verses." Ellie's shoulders hunched as she bent over the glimpses of her father's life. "Daddy tried teaching me how to say them before he went to his big ship."

Train a child up in the way she should go. *Evan never missed many teaching opportunities, did he, Lord?* "Would you mind if we shared your special gift and these verses at church tomorrow? They're hosting an event to honor Daddy." She cupped one side of her daughter's face in her open palm. "And I'd really like to display the board at his f—"

"Home-Going Celebration." Ellie bounced onto her knees. "Really, Mama?" She looked at the poster board. "You think it's good enough?"

"It's perfect." She pulled her baby girl into a hug then rocked back and forth slowly. Peace began to ease the tension in Denise's neck. Her heart pounded, as each syllable poured smoothly over her lips. "'Hear, O LORD, and be merciful to me; O LORD, be my help.' You turned my wailing into dancing; you removed my sackcloth and clothed me with joy, that my heart may sing to you and not be silent. O LORD, my God, I will give you thanks forever.' Psalm thirty, verses ten to twelve."

The two Tiptons snuggled in silence.

Denise smiled at the snapshots of her that-was-then life. She kissed her daughter's forehead, savoring the whiff of Ellie's favorite tear-free watermelon shampoo. Somehow, blocking the tears seemed scarier than letting them flow. *Hear, O LORD, and be merciful to me; O LORD, be my help.* Closing her eyes, Denise bowed her head. "Lord, thank You for comforting us with Your Word and through the gift of joyful memories."

Ellie swallowed a sob. "In Jesus' name. Amen."

Denise pressed her cheek into her daughter's curls. Evan's curls. "That's right, Baby Girl. Amen."

*Xochitl (soh-cheel) E. Dixon encourages women and teens to embrace God's grace. Her devotions will be featured in **Our Daily Bread** (www.odb.org), starting Spring 2017. She's been published in **The Upper Room, ENCOUNTER,** and **Devo 'Zine** magazines, in Inspire's **Victory, Promise** and **Forgiveness,** and at www.xedixon.com. She enjoys singing, reading, photography, and being married to her best friend, Dr. W. Alan Dixon, Sr.*

# THE CUP OF MOST EXCELLENT INEBRIATION
## Michael Faber

*You anoint my head with oil; my cup overflows.*
Psalm 23:5

Imagine after a very hard and dangerous journey, you arrive at your destination. During the journey you suffered privation and hardship. Many nights you were hungry, or at least missed the luxuries you have come to expect. Upon arrival, you are warmly greeted by the host. He hugs you, takes your coat and shows you to your seat. He takes the role of a servant and puts perfumed oil on your head, so that you can relax. You have arrived just in time for the feast! Every kind of food is set before you. As he pours you a drink, there is no rationing as you needed to do with your water on the trail. There is no hint of selfishness or holding back. Rather, laughingly, he allows the drink to run over the top, and you know there is more where that came from!

This is the image the psalmist paints for us. The time of hardship is over. The time of rejoicing and feasting has come! The LORD is a lavish host.

"What is the *cup* referred to in this verse?" The cup is a sign of the extravagant love our God holds for us. We are like wandering sheep our whole lives, and He has done everything in His power to guide us, to lead us, to protect us, and to call us home when we have gone astray. Through His Son, Jesus Christ, He laid down His life to pay the price for our sins so we could be reconciled to Him. As He hung on the cross, Jesus cried out, "I thirst."

No doubt He was physically thirsty and desired moisture for His parched lips. No doubt he longed for the cup of Thanksgiving, which He drank a few hours earlier with His beloved disciples, when He declared, "This cup is the new covenant in my blood, which is poured out for you." Luke 22:20. But He was thirsty for something more. He was thirsty for everlasting fellowship with the wandering souls who He came to save. He was thirsty for fellowship with you and me. It was for us and for our friendship He came to die.

We have spent our lifetimes wandering and looking away from Him. We have followed the lusts and passions of this world rather than our Savior, but the Good Shepherd has faithfully and longingly called us back. By the power of His grace, He has succeeded. We crossed the finish line! We have come home to His heavenly glory. We have turned to His loving embrace, and sit at His bountiful table, and now we have His cup before us. This is the cup of the new and everlasting covenant which He so graciously, so generously, and so extravagantly poured for us, to the point of overflowing! Drink from it, and there will be more. It is the joyous cup of God's most bountiful love.

But, there is more to be learned from the cup mentioned in Psalm 23. At the time of Christ and during the early Church, the Hebrew Old Testament had fallen out of use, and the Greek translation, commonly known as the *LXX*, was more commonly used. Scholars have found slight variations of wording between certain Old Testament passages in the Greek and in the Hebrew.

Modern English translations typically translate from the Hebrew scripture rather than the Greek. Therefore, sometimes the words in Scripture quoted by New Testament writers and Early Church Fathers vary somewhat from what we are used to hearing.

Psalm 23:5 is one of those places where there is a variance. In the Greek version it says something to the effect of "*your* cup inebriates most excellently."

This phrase, in the Greek translation, does bring to mind the story of Jesus at the Wedding of Cana. The host had run out of wine and Mary persuaded Jesus to save the day. He turned the water to wine, and tasting it, the guests were surprised that the host had held the most excellent wine for last. Whatever God does is always the most excellent.

The early church used the *LXX* Greek version as their old testament, so the early Church commentators spoke of this cup of inebriation.

While alcohol can relax one in a social setting and there is a certain merriment to be had while drinking, too much alcohol can be a bad thing. In general, both the Old Testament and the New Testament condemn drunkenness. See "Wine is a mocker and beer a brawler; whoever is led astray by them is not wise," Proverbs 20:1, and "Do not get drunk on wine, which leads to debauchery. Instead, be filled with the Spirit," Ephesians 5:18. The early Church Fathers saw this intoxication at the Lord's table as a good kind, not the bad kind.

A sixth-century Bishop, Fulgentius of Ruspe, opined that the drunkenness which one received from the Lord's cup "poured into the inner depths of the heart so that every affection of the heart, overcome, is assigned to oblivion." In other words, the cup helped us to abandon the things of the world that are contrary to the love of Christ and to more fully focus on Him. Theophilus, of Alexandria saw the "cup of inebriation" as one that provided exultation of immortality, and wine that eased the pains of the wounds we have suffered in this life. Bishop Ambrose saw the "cup that inebriates" as a powerful tonic to wash away every stain of sin.

I like to think of it as simply a "cup of everlasting joy." In modern times, there is a scene in Charles Dickens's *The Christmas Carol* where the ghost of Christmas Past encourages Scrooge to prepare for his upcoming spiritual journey by offering him a cup from his feast table. Scrooge drinks, and it is later revealed that this is the cup of "the milk of human kindness."

For those that have experienced intoxication from alcohol, there is a great deal of joy and mirth in that state. Unfortunately, one pays the price later with the hangover, and the possibility of alcoholism and all the pain which ensues from that condition.

The Lord's cup, however, gives us joy and a sense of wellness that comes with no ill after effects. Notice that the text only refers to the cup of "the most excellent inebriation"; it does not say this inebriation comes from alcohol. I like to think it comes straight from the Holy Spirit. Paul says, "don't be drunk on wine...instead be filled with the Spirit." Ephesians 5:18. While he doesn't say it explicitly, the Spirit brings its own exultation and joy, and sometimes even silliness, but it is the good kind of inebriation that brings only the joy without the ensuing debauchery or hangover.

Have you ever been drunk on the Holy Spirit? Has the joy of Christ ever filled you to such a degree that you are smiling, and there is an inexplicable warmth and happiness all through your being? If not, ask the LORD for another drink of His cup of most excellent inebriation, and He will surely comply.

Be filled with joy and the peace that passes all understanding!

*Michael Faber is an attorney and a Fuller Seminary graduate with a Master's Degree in Theology and Bible. His books, **The Seven Words of Jesus from the Cross, The Beatitudes According to Jesus**, and **Meditations on the Lord's Prayer**, are published in the USA, Vietnam, and India.*

# JOY DESPITE ALL
## *Judith Rose*

Living the life of a hermit is very interesting, as I am doing, thanks to a collection of autoimmune diseases, severe spinal problems and shaky hands, all due to an overactive neuron in my brain. This way of life has given me a magnificent opportunity to be so much more aware of Christ's holy presence surrounding me, loving me, and filling me with His Spirit. I have joy despite myself.

I recently wrote to a good friend that I have as many daunting problems this month as I did last, just new ones—all complex, maddening and aggravating. Still, I have been given peace and joy despite all.

The streams of creativity I experience—making gifts for my grandchildren or note cards for others, or writing my heart out in prayers and poems—have truly been flowing prayers of joyful praise. This, in turn, brings peace, joy and a very full life.

In *Chariots of Fire*, Eric Liddell said, "When I run, I feel God's pleasure." For me, when I create, I feel God's pleasure, peace, joy and energy. I might even add *healing*. It is a great gift and privilege to have the time to create a mobile—featuring knights' colorful shields—for my nine-year-old grandson, Liam. Or, to fill decorated binders with photos of my granddaughters, Camille and Chloe, age seventeen and twelve, to give to them. These are projects I could not do if I were healthy and able to work.

The time and energy I am able to spend creating with the joyful love God has placed within me is in itself prayer, worship, and divine delight in abundance. As I see the wondrous combination of colors God has created, the ideas God inspires in me, and the miraculous way He makes pictures and words work beautifully together, despite continual pain, I feel the results are miraculous. When I create, God's glory and joy is tangible.

A friend shared with me the words from a sermon reflecting on Eric Liddell's words above. "That's the purpose of our lives," the preacher said, "feeling God's pleasure and joy and sharing it with others, living in faith through joyful love."

When consciously and willingly in the arms of Christ, all is joy if I allow it to be so. This is more than the Fountain of Youth, the Hope Diamond, or the Key to All Mysteries. This is the Pearl of Great Price, the Kingdom of God itself.

God is the only answer to a life of joy and peace, whether being an ill hermit or an active athlete. God will be present to us and flow through us to others, no matter our state in life if we allow Him into our hearts and trust Him with our lives. He will use us as conduits of His loving grace and joy for others, as we nurture and share the joyous love He so generously pours upon us.

## JUDITH ROSE

❦

*Having to retire early from nursing, teaching, and water coloring due to a long list of chronic illnesses and spine problems, Judith has thoroughly enjoyed writing poems, prayers and essays, but mostly devotionals. She was delighted to discover Inspire Writers and hopes for a long relationship.*

# A HEAVENLY PERSPECTIVE

## Christine Hagion-Rzepka

"Ugggh!" I cried aloud. "Let's take a five-minute break. I'm going outside for a breather." So frustrated at the laissez-faire attitude of the musicians accompanying me in my solo, I was bound to burst if I didn't step away for a moment.

I put down my microphone more harshly than I should have, and stepped carefully over a mass of black wires that coiled around my feet like snakes. I huffed my way out of the gymnasium, which was quickly being transformed into a concert venue. I nodded politely as I passed the tech guys dressed in black and the stage hands that did who-knows-what to make everything electrical magically work together so that our music blended into sweet melodies. Theoretically, that is. Right now, the electrical guitars and the bass sounded like cats in heat on a hot summer night. And the drummer! Well, the drummer was beating out a rhythm like it was a disco song, instead of the heartfelt worshipful ballad it was supposed to be.

Taking a step outside, I breathed in deeply. The scent of the pine enveloped me, and I drank in the serenity of the sequoias that surrounded us. The tall lush trees cast a black silhouette against a postcard-perfect sky. The sun had already set in the distance, casting a purplish hue on the horizon. A few stars sparkled in the twilight. I was grateful to whoever had chosen this wonderful location for our annual Baptist Youth Convention, where our youth group was participating in a talent show. We were in such a beautiful and peaceful place, and yet I was so agitated that I might have had steam coming out of both ears.

I breathed a silent prayer: *Lord, help me calm down.* I closed my eyes and wished for the peace that passes all understanding[1], so far out of my grasp at that moment. *Peace, be still*[2], I told myself, willing it to be.

Then suddenly, I felt my body being lifted, as though I were a metal object being pulled by a powerful magnet. Without effort, I was slowly floating upward. *What is going on here?* My mind questioned: *What on earth could this be?* I wasn't dizzy. I went back through my day: *Did I eat anything today? Yes, I ate an apple a few hours ago, so it can't be low blood sugar. What is this?* I kept going higher, and below my sandaled feet I saw the cement ceiling of the gymnasium, and the dark rooftops of the other structures around the campground. The air got cooler as I ascended, and I began to feel a little chilled in the night air against my bare arms. I wished I had my sweater, which I had left back in the gymnasium.

Finally, it dawned on me: *This must be the Rapture!* I squealed with excitement at the thought. I didn't see Jesus yet, but I remembered the Scripture that we would be caught up together in the clouds to meet the Lord in the air.[3] *The joyous moment I have awaited for so long is finally coming to pass! And I am privileged to see it!* Exhilarated, I opened my eyes, eager to see all the other believers being taken up at the same time. What a joyous mid-air gathering!

But instead of seeing hundreds of others with their sandals in the sky, now that my eyes were opened, the vision ended and I was alone again, behind the gymnasium among the redwoods. I clamped my eyes shut again, wishing for a return to my reverie, like a rudely-awakened sleeper who slaps the offending alarm clock and rolls over, hoping the pleasant dream continue. But it was not to be.

I listened quietly to the sound of the crickets and gulped down the disappointment of still being on earth, but was elated at the revelation of what I had just been shown. The frustration that had overwhelmed me just minutes earlier had evaporated like a vapor, and in its place was an exuberance that could not be contained. God had answered my prayer by giving me a reminder to look at my difficult moments from a heavenly perspective.

I walked back into the gymnasium a changed young woman. I no longer cared if we placed in the talent competition. When I sang, both my heart and my voice rejoiced in animated praise. I closed my eyes and proclaimed my love and allegiance to the Master of the universe and the Maker of the moon and stars, which I had just passed on my virtual ascent into the heavens. I could almost hear the angels joining me in a chorus of exaltation and adulation to the Most High.

Now, looking back more than thirty years later, I recall that memorable day when God gave me a much-needed attitude and altitude adjustment. I smile to consider the way He can humble us in just a moment, reminding us of what is really important.

# CHRISTINE HAGION-RZEPKA

*Christine Hagion-Rzepka writes poetry, blogs, research, inspiring sermons and investigative features for magazines and professional newsletters. Her work has also appeared in* **Chicken Soup for the Soul** *and various Inspire titles. She serves as a guest reviewer for* **Health Promotion Practice** *and the* **Journal of Family Violence**, *both peer-reviewed academic journals.*

[1] *...and the peace of God, which passeth all understanding, will guard your hearts and minds through Christ Jesus.*
(Philippians 4:7, KJV)

[2] *And he arose, and rebuked the wind, and said unto the sea, Peace, be still. And the wind ceased, and there was a great calm.*
(Mark 4:39, KJV)

[3] *For the Lord himself shall descend from heaven with a shout, with the voice of the archangel, and with the trump of God: and the dead in Christ shall rise first: Then we which are alive and remain shall be caught up together with them in the clouds, to meet the Lord in the air: and so shall we ever be with the Lord.*
(1 Thessalonians 4:16–17, KJV)

# THE JOY OF DISNEY

## *Sydney Smalling*

Rose hurried up the sidewalk, her pale pink dress billowing out behind her as she ran. It was July 17, 1955. It was the day she had looked forward to for months.

The crowd moved towards Harbor Blvd. People were talking to each other, their voices filled with excitement. Rose stopped in the middle of the sidewalk and looked up.

High above her head, a large white sign stood, sparkling in the sunlight. It read, *Disneyland.* Her heart felt like it was going to beat out of her chest from happiness.

The day had finally arrived.

Rose turned, peered into the crowd of people, and saw the auburn hair of her sister, Madeline.

She stood and waited for her amidst the crowd. Rose's feet begged to run down the path, and into the park that Walt Disney created.

Madeline caught up to her, but she barely noticed. Rose looked over in the direction of the park. Over the roofs of buildings, she could see the tall spires of the castle.

Soon their parents caught up to them, along with their eleven-year-old brother, Tom. They continued their walk towards the park.

"Are you excited?" A voice came from her right, jarring her out of her daydream.

Her sister, Madeline, stared at her, with an expression mixed with joy and exhilaration. Rose was sure that her expression matched exactly.

"Of course," Rose replied. "I've never felt so excited in my life!"

After a few more minutes of walking, they reached a ticket booth. Five tickets later, they walked into Disneyland.

They stopped and stared in amazement. The train station was beautifully decorated with flags and banners and a large Mickey Mouse made of flowers. All around them, people talked excitedly, and laughter sounded all around.

"Well," her father said after a moment. "We haven't come all this way to stare at the front gates."

They walked into the park—staring with awe and wonder at everything they saw—down a long street with buildings on each side, singing and laughter all around.

Although there were many people on the street, Rose barely noticed them. She stared straight ahead at the large castle at the end of the road.

Rose and her family walked forward through the crowd. A group of people was gathering in a circle-shape end of the street.

In the center of the circle stood Walt Disney.

He was surrounded by reporters, and held a small piece of paper in his hand.

After a minute or two, Walt stepped up to the microphones. A hush fell over the crowd.

"To all who come to this happy place; welcome," he said. "Disneyland is your land. Here age relives fond memories of the past...and here youth may savor the challenge and promise of the future. Disneyland is dedicated to the ideas, the dreams, and the hard facts that have created America...with the hope that it will be a source of joy and inspiration to all the world."

The crowd erupted in cheers. Rose's father leaned over and kissed his wife. Madeline and Tom grinned from ear to ear, and jumped up and down with excitement.

All around them, people were cheering so loudly, and were so happy. There wasn't a frowning face in the whole park.

And Rose was full of joy.

❦

*Sydney Smalling is a student at a Christian School in California. She loves to read, write, and hang out with her friends. Sydney has two cats, whom she likes to play with. She also loves to visit Disneyland annually, and hopes to be a professional author when she's older.*

# ONCE UPON A CASTLE

## *Dee Aspin*

The clouds forming in my mind defied the beauty of the Bavarian countryside.

*What's going on down here? Where are you God? Do you see us?*

Five years earlier, I had crawled through depression in nursing school. When faced with various levels of human suffering, I doubted. *Who am I? Why am I here?*

I clung to Christ and the Bible daily, to forge my path to graduation and blue skies.

Now, as I hosteled through Europe on an extended backpack adventure with yet another new travel companion, the fog reappeared.

So many youth my age crisscrossed country lines on the Eurail, without work or ambition. No limits to drugs, alcohol, even sex, for many. The lifeless churches I infrequently attended offered only religion without the life-giving Spirit I depended on.

One memorable Sunday I begged, "Lord, I have to talk to a Christian, a *real* believer. I feel confused." Tears tipped my lids and reached the map sprawled below me on my dorm bunk.

*I haven't spoken to a believer since I left California. I thought I'd be fine, just me and You, God. I was at first, but six weeks in, Lord, I never realized how much I need Christian fellowship. I've never been without it.*

I dropped postcards to parents or friends every week. No one wrote back. I never knew where I'd be. Phone calls were expensive, and I was on $15-a-day budget. Cell phones didn't exist.

One Monday morning, I headed out for an acclaimed tour to the Neuschwanstein Castle. Ironically, the daunting majestic structure Crazy Ludwig built for his love, belied the tragic course of their relationship. She drowned in the icy blue waters adjacent to the castle. The story behind the opulence cast a further shadow on my fragile state. Wealth, beauty, even extravagant love, does not bring purpose or meaning to life.

Afterwards, I walked the long winding path from the castle and crossed the street with other travelers to the bus stop. We had just missed it. *Two hours until the next bus?* I griped as much as any.

We all shuffled into the guest house to pass the time. I ordered a sandwich and water. Shallow chatter erupted here and there, the length of our long benched table where tourists from all around the globe sat and rested. The aroma of fresh brewed German beer and the sight of foamy mugs lightened the atmosphere.

A middle-aged man and his wife seated across from me told a story of their baby kangaroo in distinct Australian accents. We all laughed as they shared vignettes, the nuisance, and antics of raising a *joey* to maturity.

Conversation lulled, then shifted. Someone mentioned a recent troubling world news event. The man's tone lowered, "People often live life misguided. They blow out a candle, their conscience, and then try to use it to guide them through the darkness."

His comment inspired peace—my spirit settled. *There is something different and familiar about this man and his wife.*

"Are you a Christian?" The question popped out as easily as my tears emerged.

"Yes, I'm a pastor. What's wrong?" His clear blue eyes searched mine.

"I prayed yesterday that God would send me a Christian." The background chatter seemed to mute. I still couldn't believe my ears as I processed the profound realization God was answering me.

The man spoke a word to his wife, walked around the table and sat next to me.

"What's the matter?" He searched my face.

"I don't know. Yesterday I told God I needed to talk to a Christian. I've been travelling for six weeks and there's so much stuff in the world. I am feeling confused."

The pastor talked to me about life and purpose. Verses. Meaning. About our Christian faith. I don't remember all he said until his final words.

"Denise, we used to think the sun revolved around the earth, but we were wrong. The Earth revolves around the sun. And in our Christian faith, that is the order of our lives. Jesus is to be at the center—our lives revolve around Him—not the other way around. He is the Son of God. We live to serve and please Him as our Creator. Reminders are all around.

"When we look up at the sky, He is the Light of the World. When we look at the mountains, He is the rock of Gibralter. If we look at the flowers, He is the Lily of the Valley and the Rose of Sharon. Wherever we look in life, we will see Him there. Even in the midst of the darkest night, He is the Bright and Morning Star—the last star that brings in the light of a new day. We are meant to keep our eyes on Him. To trust Him and remember He is always present."

Words of life and truth anchored my soul and faith to the dock of serenity. I felt unspeakable joy. Though surrounded by people, God heard me when I felt alone in a desert. He strengthened my faith and provided strength to last the rest of that journey and beyond. Because He answered my lone prayer so specifically, I could not deny His love or existence. No matter how many questions remain unanswered in the world we live in—He sees it all.

*Dee Aspin is a writer, speaker, author of **Lord of the Ringless**, an audie nominated faith-based devotional and **Dogspirations**. Dee lives with her husband, Steve, and mini-schnauzer, Benji. She's written for CBN.com, Guideposts, Revel and Barbour Book's compilations tbr 2016; **3-Minute Devotions for a Dog-Lover's Heart**, and **3-Minute Devotions for a Cat-Lover's Heart**.* Her website is http://deeaspin.com/

# Jane's Contagious Joy

## (A Short Tribute)

### *Mary Allen*

My sister-in-law, Jane, had cancer, again. She had beat breast cancer several years ago, and we all did a collective sigh of relief. But this time, her doctors at the university hospital sent her home to die. The cancer nudged its way through her body until it took over almost every part of her. But it couldn't push out the joy God poured into Jane.

We knew she was going to die. We'd known it for a while. I went to see her to say goodbye when she felt death was imminent. "I don't want to wait until you die to fly out for a funeral or send flowers. I want to spend time with you, Jane." We prayed that she would make it long enough for me to see her alive.

It was a thoroughly wonderful trip—too short—but a blessing, regardless. We laughed, we cried and we shared our hearts about God. "I'm not afraid to die," Jane said. She was looking forward to seeing Jesus. Her faith remained strong, her joy evident, and as always, she inspired me.

Before I left, she received word from her oncologist there was a new treatment that could add about a year to her life. The treatment made her feel better. So good, in fact that she and my brother, Chuck, took a trip in a little trailer to spend some quality time together. She was able to see her sister Marilyn, her brother Chuck (not to be confused with her husband, my brother Chuck) and her best friends, Mel and Jan. And, I was blessed to see her again when she and my brother stopped by to see me and my husband, Bob. The four of us went out to dinner, and had such a great time together, laughing and acting crazy. It was a memory in the making. "You look so good, Jane. It is hard to believe you are so sick."

"I'm glad to be having a good day. I almost forgot I was sick, too," she said with a smile. Her joy overflowed from her heart and absorbed right into mine. Two weeks later, my brother cut the trip short and flew her home because she was not feeling well.

It wasn't too many days later when Chuck called to tell me she had slipped into eternity. "She died peacefully," he shared. No surprise there. Nevertheless, my eyes spilled over with tears, and my words became lodged in the back of my throat. Losing someone you care for so deeply is difficult. But, I'm thankful she died with her daughters, Beth, Jodi, and Allison, and my brother Chuck at her side. I know as Jane let go of Chuck's hand, she reached for the hand of her Savior.

Her laughter will forever sing in my memory like a beautiful melody. Her joy-filled smile will continually encourage my heart. Her words will remain an inspiration on my journey through life. Jane's spirit is with Jesus, but the memory of her remains firmly planted within me.

I have given considerable thought to my feelings concerning her death, and I know her family will miss her tremendously. That is normal and to be expected. But, I don't believe we are overcome with waves of grief and sorrow. I think of how much I love her, how much she means to me, the encouragement she always poured into my heart, and the long conversations we shared. Yes, I am sad, but overwhelmed with peace and a joy that is completely unfathomable to my finite mind. Tears will flow freely when my heart takes that unexpected turn toward sorrow, but I know Jane was a gift from God to me from the time I was fourteen years old. I had four older brothers and when Chuck married her, I was thrilled—finally a precious sister! And that is what she will remain to me—*for always.*

I've wondered if it is normal to be so at peace with a loved one's death, as I am not drowning in waves of debilitating grief. But I have come to the conclusion that the legacy of my sweet sister should not be one of grief at her passing, but of rejoicing in the life she lived and shared with me and so many others. I will rejoice in the gift God gave me of her, and the part she played in my life's journey. I will rejoice in what Jane taught me, how she blessed me, and where she brought me. I don't want to grieve her departure from this world, but to find the great joy in her beautiful memory. I may not understand why God chose to release her from her earthly body, but I will trust His decision. Someday, I, too, will depart this world, and I really don't want my loved ones to sorrow in my death, but to find joy in my life—the same way I found joy in Jane's life and her journey Home.

This is Mary Allen's third story for an Inspire Anthology. Her first book, **Crying in the Morgue, Laughing in the Dark**, is meant to inspire people to find purpose and joy in their own lives. "We are treasures to God. We need to see ourselves the way He sees us."

# THE JOYFUL GETAWAY

## *Solomon Gee*

Nate smiled as he hung the phone back in the cradle. His heart bounced inside. *How will I keep this secret? I have to try so this is the best surprise she's ever had.* For this surprise, cancer—the unwanted guest—needed to take a backseat.

He planned a twenty-second anniversary trip at the Ritz Carlton in Half Moon Bay, California. He helped her pack a light bag for a two-night stay. For this trip, the cost didn't matter. Every detail needed to add to the experience, just in case.

Driving the scenic route allowed her to take in the unfolding landscape. Coming through the tunnel of trees, they gasped at the beauty in front of them. Against the backdrop of the blue sky and sunlight, the white-foamed caps of the waves crashed against the saw-tooth cliffs of Half Moon Bay.

Jean smiled. "I love the ocean. It brings back so many fond memories."

Nate drove up the cobblestone drive and under the awning of the hotel's shiny brass entrance. The hostess escorted them to the front counter introducing them to the concierge while the valet unloaded the suitcases and parked the car. When the luggage cart arrived at the front desk, the hostess turned to Nate and Jean and with a smile she said, "Enjoy your special stay."

Slab-tiled floors, accented by marble pillars and polished redwood furniture worthy of royalty, greeted them. The bellhop stopped in front of their room and slid the key card to open the door. Jean's fast-paced steps took her to the window. She pulled it open to welcome the familiar sights and sounds. Nate stepped up to her back wrapping his arms around her. She leaned against him.

"This is my safe place," Jean said as she wiped her cheek.

Her attention turned to the right of the window. She noticed a round table, holding fully opened yellow tulips—her favorite flowers. Jean's gaze dropped to the bottom of the vase. She picked up the framed wedding portrait and recent photo of their family vacationing. Tears streamed down her face. These two images depicted their lives, what they had accomplished as a couple and as parents. Twenty-two years summarized between two pictures.

When it was time for dinner, Nate asked her to change into comfortable clothes.

"We're going to dine in the hotel restaurant."

"I'm so excited," Jean said. "This feels like a second honeymoon."

Nate's smile opened wide.

"Wow. This is exactly what I'd hoped for. I want to take your mind off everything else, at least for a couple of days." Taking her hand, he led her to the restaurant.

Nate checked in with the host, who seated them at a cozy booth looking out toward the ocean and the setting sun. As the waiter introduced himself, he asked Jean what type of tea she would prefer.

Her eyebrows lifted and eyes widened as she smiled first at the waiter, then at her husband.

Nate then knew the staff would take care of Jean's dietary needs. He sighed.

The waiter left their table to get the drinks. Jean and Nate held hands and prayed for their meal. When they looked toward the window, the orange disc, seeming to hang over the water, cast a glow across the ocean's surface. They didn't need many words as they held hands and watched the sun sink.

"Look what God did," Jean said.

"He hasn't forgotten us," Nate responded. "It doesn't hurt that it's romantic, too." He grinned.

As the outside light faded, the couple admired the chandeliers and the mood they continued to maintain. They laughed, shared stories, and kept the conversation in high spirits.

"Nate, always remember this night."

He struggled to find his voice. "Always."

The next morning, the sunlight shone through the large white slats of the New England style window coverings.

"After breakfast, let's explore the grassy courtyard until time for our spa session," Nate said.

They held hands as they strolled admiring the vegetation. As they walked, Jean named every bit of foliage they saw.

"How do you remember what all these plants are? You never studied them in school. You even know their botanical names."

"I don't know. Somehow, I have a knack for it," Jean said.

They headed to the spa and their separate locker rooms. They each received monogrammed robes and slippers as the attendants gave directions to where they would enjoy their massages. As soon as the session began, Jean closed her eyes and her breathing slowed into a steady rhythm.

Nate chattered to anyone who listened. A few moments later, Jean opened one eye and looked across at him.

"Shhh."

"Oops, I'm sorry," he said closing his eyes.

Nate woke up as the masseuses said goodbye.

They remained unmoving fifteen minutes longer breathing in the smell. Somehow, the oils blended to create a citrus-like fragrance.

Later, Jean and Nate met back at the spa's lobby where cups of ice-cold water with lemon slices were waiting for them. They sat together sipping the refreshing drinks.

After wandering back to their room, Nate opened the door to the smell of roses wafting towards them. Yellow petals formed the shape of a large heart on the mattress. Nate appreciated all the hotel staff did in creating this affectionate mood.

Since they still had daylight, they changed their clothes and went outside to enjoy the garden, the golf course, and most of all, the beach scenery. Along their walk, they often stopped to take pictures adding to the fun with crazy faces and poses. Their temporary seclusion from reality was the ideal second honeymoon environment they had hoped for.

As the chill of the evening set in, Jean and Nate held onto each other a bit tighter while a helpful passerby snapped a few photos of them. So many thoughts ran through Nate's mind as he held his bride.

"When you find out your cancer is gone, we'll come back again," Nate said.

"I would love that," Jean said.

As Jean turned to face Nate she said, "Let's stay outside a little bit longer and watch the sunset."

"Gladly, my dear." Nate embraced her.

"I feel so secure when you wrap your arms around me."

Returning to their room, Nate started a warm bath so Jean could relax in the deep, Jacuzzi, marbled tub. Later, a warm towel draped around her, Jean looked out the window.

"I love how the moon's light reflects on the water. It looks somewhat like wisps of floating clouds. I can hear the crashing waves outside the window," Jean said.

They heard a knock at the door. "Room service."

Nate smiled as he opened the textured, wooden entry. Moments later, they enjoyed their evening meal in front of the glowing fireplace, which provided the perfect, romantic setting.

Later, they retired for the evening among the rose petals while the ocean provided the soothing background sound to help them fall asleep. Nate held Jean in his arms silently wishing they could enjoy one more day in this paradise.

Though they knew her body continued to betray her, the weekend reminded them of the deep, joyful love they shared as husband and wife. Tomorrow, once again, they would face the cancer treatments. Nevertheless, tonight was theirs.

*Solomon Gee lives in Vacaville, California with his wife, Kathleen, their youngest son, and an indoor cat. This short story is an excerpt from his recent book,* **Every Day Passes Is One Day Closer**. *His website is* www.CourageToLiveOn.com

# Rescue

## *Suzan Kneedler*

In May 2010, a San Jose mountain in Chile collapsed. A crew of thirty-three miners barely escaped death by rushing down 2,300 feet into a refuge. The gold and copper mine, in operation for 111 years, had excavated the mountain into a honeycomb of tunnels. It was doomed to collapse. When it gave way, it dropped a seventy-ton boulder straight down to the bottom. It rested directly over the refuge.

When the dust cleared, the miners surveyed the situation. A head count assured all thirty-three made it alive with no serious injury. Then they calculated resources. The refuge was supposed to have everything necessary to keep thirty men alive for three days. What they found was disheartening.

The radio for communication didn't function, stairs in the airshaft failed to reach the surface, and the food larder had been raided down to only several cans of tuna, boxes of crackers, and quarts of milk. Meager fare even for three days, they consumed only an ounce of tuna broth and a single cracker every twenty-four hours.

Above ground, news of the collapse spread and a crowd gathered at the mine to hear news of father, son, husband, neighbor, and friend. A defensive member of mine management told them the mountain was too unstable to deploy search and rescue, and to go home to wait for more news.

When they refused to leave, guards threatened them with weapons. They called the media and the news stirred up such an outcry, the government sent an agent to oversee the rescue effort. The military erected a tent city for 300 family members including a medical clinic, school, and mess hall. An army of reporters and curiosity-seekers surrounded the compound.

Below, the men sweltered in ninety-degree heat and humidity. Flashlight and helmet beams were losing power. Unable to communicate to the team above, they struggled to believe they would survive, and began to pray.

Above, the location of the refuge was known, but the boulder prevented direct access. Heavy-duty drill teams were brought in from other mines in Chile, Australia, and the United States, but none could successfully drill around the massive boulder. After two weeks of drilling around the clock, further effort seemed futile. Even if they were successful in getting through, there was little hope of finding the men alive. A quiet despair lay over the camp. Mourning began to replace hope.

Then it happened. A wild idea inspired one last valiant effort. What would have been scorned earlier became a brilliant idea—and the key that unlocked the door. With hope against hope, the drill pierced the roof of the refuge on day seventeen.

Hearing the sound, but groggy and emaciated, the miners were slow to respond. Using what little strength they had, they spray painted the shaft of the drill, knowing the mark would be recognized as a sign of life. Next the men tied a piece of cloth above the drill head, with a written message saying they were all alive. Then they pounded on the pipe. Noise ascended, and so did the drill.

When the marked drill bit reached the surface, everyone—engineer, driller, family, friend, reporter, and observer—shouted in wild celebration. The men were alive!

Tubes sent down through the narrow borehole contained a camera and microphone for communication, food, clothing, medicine, and mail. But the miners could not come up. A much wider shaft would have to be drilled to get them out—and that took another fifty-nine days.

The wait was almost unbearable. Everyone had to hang tight both below and above to be reunited. The men below vowed to walk out, proud to be miners, united as one crew. They were ready to face whatever waited for them on the surface.

A capsule designed to lift a single rider was engineered and lowered by cable through the larger shaft. On the sixty-ninth day the first man was raised to the surface. Tears of joy and relief, with shouts of victory and elation, filled the air as each of the thirty-three miners emerged.

One of the greatest news stories of the decade serves as a powerful illustration of the Gospel of Salvation. When life collapses and we're trapped in our small, dark oppressive world, we need rescue. When hope turns to mourning, we begin to pray. God hears and begins to bore the truth of His love deep into our soul. He opens the way for us to be reunited with Him.

Through the capsule of Salvation, we are raised to new life. With tears flowing freely and shouts of victory, our soul knows the joy of being rescued.

❦

*Suzi Kneedler lives with her husband, Pete, in Carmichael, California. She enjoys her grown children and their spouses, grandchildren, and pets.*

# The Joy Set Before Him
## *Tracilynn Rodrigues*

What does joy mean to you? Most people would probably agree with the dictionary's definition: "Joy is a feeling of happiness that comes from success, good fortune, or a sense of well-being." But, how does this definition stand Biblically?

Paul wrote, *Looking unto Jesus, the author and finisher of our faith; who for the joy set before Him endured the cross, despising the shame, and is set down at the right hand of the throne of God.* (Hebrew 12:2, KJV)

In Acts, we see that after the apostles were beaten and then released, *They departed from the presence of the council, rejoicing that they were counted worthy to suffer shame for His name.* (Acts 5:41, KJV)

Peter declared, *Beloved, think it not strange concerning the fiery trial which is to try you...but rejoice, inasmuch as you are partakers of Christ's sufferings; that, when His glory will be revealed, you may be glad also with exceeding joy.* (1 Peter 4:12–13, KJV)

How could extensive suffering, such as the cross, bring Jesus joy? This verse lets us know that though there wasn't joy in the moment, He endured the cross because He focused on a future joy that would come as a result. What did Jesus focus on?

You might say, "Salvation, or us."

That was only a small portion of His joy. Though His joy included you and me, He had something much bigger in mind. He had His eyes set on a wedding—His. Ever since the earth's creation, Jesus longed for a mate. The animals had mates, Adam had Eve, but there wasn't another of Jesus's kind for Him. The cross made a way for us to become new creations in Him. We have the privilege to be formed into His image, if we yield to the promptings of the Holy Spirit. Thus, making us fit to be His bride.

So, also for us, we can find joy in suffering, knowing this is temporary and it works something greater in us—forming us into His image so we can partake of the wedding as His bride.

I like the promise in Nehemiah 8:10 (KJV). The people wept before the Lord after they heard the words of the law, knowing they had come short of living up to them. Nehemiah and the priests comforted the people by telling them to rejoice, *for the joy of the Lord is your strength.*

Does happiness strengthen you during a trial? Most likely, no. It is an emotion that comes and goes based on your circumstances. But joy can give you strength in the midst of your trial, because it is much deeper than an emotion.

Years ago, I read *Maria* by Eugenia Price. One line stuck with me ever since. "Joy, real joy, true joy, is God in the marrow of your bones."

The Bible declares that the life is in the blood (Leviticus 17:11). And blood is formed in the marrow of our bones. This life substance reaches to every area of our bodies. If our joy is God Himself, in the deepest place of our being where life is formed daily and flows out to the rest of our being, then nothing can shake our joy.

He is not only my present joy, but an even greater joy is set before my eyes. It is the day I dance with Him at the greatest wedding celebration in history.

What about you? Is He your source of joy? No matter what trial you face today, let His joy sustain you, and give you a future and a hope. Look beyond the limitations of this world.

Put on your dancing shoes, and let the King of Glory sweep you off your feet.

*Tracilynn Rodrigues believes "A word fitly spoken (or written) is like apples of gold in pictures of silver." (Proverbs 25:11, KJV) It is her desire to be a pen in the Master Writer's hand.*

# HAVE SOME FAITH

## *Lisa Braxton*

"I don't have a father," the little boy said in a barely audible voice. "I don't know my father at all."

The other children seated with Qu'Amere at the arts-and-crafts table met eyes with him. After an awkward silence, they looked away and returned to the coloring activity I had given them. They didn't know what to say, and neither did I. I was a new Sunday school teacher in the town where I grew up. Now, I was back after years of working in other parts of the country as a television news reporter. Still single and in my mid-30s, I'd come home because the regional cable news station in the area offered me the evening news anchor position—a step up from the reporting jobs I'd had.

Soon after settling into an apartment, I began attending services at the church I grew up in—a thriving institution in a blighted neighborhood. The church was looking for Sunday school teachers and I raised my hand to volunteer. I envisioned teaching kids on the junior high or high school level. In the past, with each career move, I'd done volunteer work with teenagers in the towns I'd lived in. This had helped me to get to know the people and the community I'd be reporting on, and feel like I was making a contribution.

To prepare me for this new challenge, the church put me through a lengthy training program, which concluded with a weekend regional Sunday school teachers' workshop to learn how to make Bible lessons fun. The Sunday I returned after completing my training, the director of Christian education invited me into her office.

"The first grade teacher quit," she said. "Apparently she was burned out and wants to be in class instead of teaching one. The timing is perfect for you to step in. I'd like to assign you to that class."

I asked her to repeat what she'd said to make sure I had heard her correctly. I'd assumed she'd called me in to hear more about the workshop, not to assign me to a class right away—especially not a class of kids that young.

"But I don't have experience with kids that age," I said, as my heart rate picked up. "They might not feel comfortable with me."

She smiled. "Don't worry. You won't be on your own. You'll have an assistant."

Speaking in front of a group of children was much different than broadcasting the news into a television camera lens. My voice trembled with nervousness, and I had a dry mouth during the first few Sundays. It reminded me of the times I had to make speeches in front of my class in high school. However, I followed the lesson exactly as it appeared in the teacher's handbook as if it was a life preserver. And in time, I began to feel more at ease and developed a rapport with my students. I reinforced the Bible teachings, utilizing what I had learned in the weekend training workshop: Christian games, puzzles, music, cartoons, and arts and crafts. It was reassuring to have my assistant—a high school student—always there to make sure the kids didn't get distracted.

But nothing could have prepared me for Qu'Amere, the six-year-old who'd experienced so much pain in his young life, and who shared his feelings with his Sunday school classmates. I prayed for Qu'Amere and looked for guidance from God on how I could help the little boy. I felt that God was leading me to reach out to him.

"You two have a good time," Qu'Amere's grandmother shouted after us, as I took him by the hand and walked to my car on a bitterly cold Saturday afternoon. I'd gotten her permission to take him to Christmas Village to meet Santa, the elves, and real reindeer that were staying at the zoo next to the Village. As I buckled Qu'Amere into the backseat, I wondered if I was taking on more than I could handle. I wouldn't have my assistant there for support as I did at church, and there'd be no other children to keep Qu'Amere company. I was on my own.

On our way to Christmas Village, I struggled to make conversation.

"How's school?" I asked him.

"Okay," he responded.

"Do you have a lot of friends?"

He gave me a shrug.

The conversation went much the same later over burgers. By the time I returned him to his grandmother, I was drained. Being an effective communicator was central to my career, but with

Qu'Amere, I felt inept. I had wanted to take away his sadness about his father's absence from his life for one afternoon, but I felt I had failed. Maybe I had misunderstood the direction in which God was leading me. Maybe He wanted me to simply continue praying for Qu'Amere and provide him with the best Biblical teaching I could, through the Sunday school lessons.

Then one day, after church, his grandmother approached me.

"My grandson really enjoyed the time he spent with you," she said, her eyes twinkling. "That's all he's been talking about with his little friends. Thank you for picking him up."

Initially, I wondered if she was being gracious, trying to spare the feelings of the well-meaning, but clueless person I was when it came to interacting with children—until the day Qu'Amere stayed after class to help me put away the craft supplies. "When are we going somewhere again?" he said. "That was a lot of fun."

Qu'Amere and I became buddies, hanging out a couple of Saturday afternoons a month. I learned that the best way to have a conversation with Qu'Amere, was to let him talk when he was ready. On our way to the skating rink, aquarium, arcade, or matinee, he'd tell me jokes that brought me to tears, or say how mean his teachers were, and try to convince me it was only fair that *they* go to school, too, and be assigned homework. He'd share stories about his yellow Labrador named Cinnamon, and describe, scene-by-scene, the scary movies he watched with his grandmother until I'd beg him to change the subject—I grew frightened just hearing about them! Eventually he opened up about a more serious subject—his father. Qu'Amere did in fact know his father, but said he'd only been around him a few times.

His grandmother, aunts, and uncles marveled at how well behaved Qu'Amere was when he was with me. Sometimes, a few hours before I was scheduled to pick him up, I'd get a phone call from his grandmother canceling our plans because he'd acted up at school and was on punishment. He'd gotten a reputation for being bad, talking back to his teacher. I didn't understand why, though, he never misbehaved with me.

One day after he was taken off a recent punishment, Qu'Amere climbed into my car, shoulders slumped and shaking his head. "You're the only one who understands me," he said, his voice breaking. He sounded beleaguered, much more mature than the seven-year-old he now was. I swallowed hard to push down the lump in my throat, and began to realize how much he valued my presence in his life.

When we got in line at the bowling alley to rent our shoes, a man recognized me from watching the cable news station. He came over to us and shook my hand.

"What's it like to be on TV?" Qu'Amere asked as the man walked away.

I thought about telling him fascinating stories about interviewing politicians and celebrities or riding floats in local parades, but instead decided to turn the question into an opportunity. "You can find out for yourself," I said.

Qu'Amere cocked his head to the side and narrowed his eyes at me. "How can I do that?"

"You could be on television if you wanted."

He laughed. "That'll never happen."

The cable station had recently launched a pet show. Local residents were invited into the studio to be interviewed with their pets. I arranged for Qu'Amere to come on the show with Cinnamon. A few days after the show aired, I took him to a park for inline skating. As a skater whizzed past us, he spun around and shouted, "I've seen you on TV!"

"Wow! He recognized me," Qu'Amere said, beaming. I was fairly sure the skater was referring to me, but I decided not to point that out.

"How does it feel to be a celebrity?" I asked.

He pumped his fists in the air as he skated along, "I feel great. Like a million bucks."

I understood what Qu'Amere was saying—I, too, felt like a million bucks. I had discovered fulfillment volunteering with children, but made all the richer by a little boy who helped me see that all I had to do was have some faith in order to make a difference.

A shorter version in fall 2015 issue of *The Northwestern* (Northwestern University Alumni Magazine)

# LISA BRAXTON

*Lisa Braxton earned her MFA in Creative Writing from Southern New Hampshire University, and M.S. in journalism from Northwestern University. She has won awards for her work in television and as well in literary writing. She is seeking representation for her first novel. Her website is* www.lisabraxton.com

# To Walk in Your Joy
## *Kelly Madden*

Lord, help me to slow down

To hear Your voice

To know Your will

In the midst of my busy schedule

And in the middle of my worries and cares.


Help me, Lord, to choose to sit at Your feet

With open ears and a willing heart,

A heart pliable for You to mold.

Teach me what it means to rest in You

And to walk in Your joy.

*Kelly Madden is married, has two daughters, and two granddaughters. She started His Word Publications in 1995, self-publishing two books, **Getting God's Perspective** (1998) and **Talk With Jesus** (2005). Kelly has published numerous writings in past anthologies by Inspire Press, and also in **A New Heart** magazine.*

# JOY IN PSALM 81

## *Kris Lindsay*

*There it is...again.* I looked up from my Bible and sighed, then looked back down at the little word that taunted me—*joy*.

The first line of Psalm 81 said to sing for joy. But I didn't *feel* like being joyful, or singing. I rarely did. Besides, it was laundry and grocery-shopping day, and I was all set to plow through and get things done. Trudge mode felt comfortable.

I read on.

*Oh great, verse 4 says singing for joy is a command, not an option.*

I leaned back and crossed my arms. I couldn't just "be joyful." Especially with nothing happy going on. Still, God said I had to do it...

*What if I took it by faith that today is going to be a good day?*

My chest tightened and my heart screamed, "No, don't do it!"

Uh oh...why was I afraid to think good things would happen?

*Because something bad might happen instead. How can I possibly know if it's a good day until the events actually unfold?*

Yeah, wasn't it safer to just wait and see if good things happened? That way I wouldn't be disappointed if they didn't.

But then I took inventory of my mood and realized I felt lousy. On this ordinary day, with nothing bad going on, my muscles were all tense and achy. I felt listless and glum, like I was walking through a dimly lit trench.

*I don't like living this way. I really do want to live on a higher, joy-filled plain.*

Okay, I reasoned that technically every day was a good day for those who love God because, even when bad things happen, God works those things to good. Romans 8:28 said so.

I decided I'd try to believe that every day would be a good day with God by my side. To do this, I would do two things:

- Say to myself, "It's a good day."

- Read Psalm 81.

And I'd keep doing this every day until God's joy finally sunk in…hopefully.

The next morning, I told myself, *It's a good day.*

Hope brightened my heart for a second, then fear snuffed it out.

I opened my Bible to Psalm 81 and started reading.

When I got to the end of verse 10, my stomach knotted and my arms pressed into my sides. It said, "Open wide your mouth and I will fill it." I pictured a baby bird with its beak open as wide as it could, waiting expectantly for a tasty morsel to drop in from heaven.

Why was it so hard for me to open my mouth wide and believe God would fill it? Why was it so hard to say, "It's going to be a good day," and believe God had good things in store for me?

Maybe it was because of my past. Many years ago I went through a tough time where one bad thing after another happened. Sickness, isolation, trauma. And plenty of hard things had happened to me since. Maybe I was defensively wary of the future because of past experience. Maybe I didn't want to let my guard down and get broadsided again.

I looked back at two verses I'd just read. Verses 6 and 7 talked about how God had removed the Israelite's burden and rescued them from slavery in Egypt.

Hope flickered again as I thought back on my tough times and remembered how God had removed burden after burden from my shoulders, too. I couldn't even count the times He'd rescued me and brought me through.

*Yes, You are the LORD my God, Who has always been there for me.*

Then I thought back on my life and remembered all the fantastically *good* things I'd received—so many that I couldn't count them, either. Maybe I felt I'd had my share of blessings and didn't deserve more.

Whatever the reason, I wanted to get unstuck. I wanted my arms to break free from my sides and open wide to take in all the good things Heaven had for me.

But *open* felt scary. Risky. Vulnerable. How did I know God would bless me with good things on any given day? Maybe He would, but maybe He wouldn't. Besides, wouldn't assuming an unlimited supply of blessings be rudely presumptuous?

Well…no. My heart lightened. God *will* provide blessings for me each day *because He loves me.* He is my beloved and I am His (Song of Solomon 6:3). I am His precious child, as are all who put their trust in Him (John 1:12). Because of what Jesus did on the cross, we believers are totally righteous and accepted by our adoring Heavenly Father. Jesus loves us so much that He gave His life so we could be together forever. Of course, He would want to give us good gifts.

As I thought about it, I realized God does, in fact, provide me with good things every hour of every day. I just usually take them for granted…until they're gone. Last winter, due to a mishap, we were without propane for a few days. With no heater, we bundled up in front of our minimal fireplace to keep the chill off. But what we really missed was our hot water. I wasn't about to step under a shower of cold winter water. I didn't fully appreciate my hot water until I didn't have it anymore.

And awhile back, I hurt my shoulder. I could still do most things, but I couldn't put my coat on by myself. A couple of times I had to go out in the cold with my coat slung across my back, which only kept half of me warm. I'd never thought to be thankful for healthy deltoid muscles, or thousands of other parts and functions of my body that *were* working well and didn't hurt.

God had been providing so many good things for me every day. The Bible says God will never leave or forsake us (Deuteronomy 31:6). What made me think He would stop?

God loves us and wants to shower us with good things, and will. And when bad things happen, as they often do, God will be there to rescue us, help us through, and work the situations to good. What was so scary about that?

I took a deep breath. My stomach eased a bit.

As I continued reading Psalm 81 every day, I noticed my optimism increasing and my mood getting brighter. The truth of God's word pried open the door of my heart a little more each day.

After reading this Psalm four or five times a week for nine months, here is what it says to me:

Sing for joy to God, who is my strength.

This is a command—not an option—because God *wants* His children to be full of joy.

And why shouldn't I be?

God says, "I removed the burdens of your sins, hurts, and responsibilities from your shoulders. I set you free from your tasks—let me do the work. And remember all those times you were in trouble? You called out and I heard and rescued you. I am the Lord your God who brought you through all your hard times. Open wide your mouth and I will fill it with every good thing you need and more. If you won't listen and yield to Me, I'll let you stubbornly follow your own devices and schemes. But if you'll just listen to Me and follow My ways, how quickly

I'll subdue the enemy of your soul and quench your insecurities and fears. On top of that, I'll give you My best; I'll satisfy and sweeten your life with Jesus."

Let God's joy sink in!

Previously published on Kris's website.

*The desire of Kris's heart is to grow closer and closer to Jesus, and to help others do the same. She enjoys discipling new Christians, and spending time with family and friends. Read more about her journey to find greater peace and healing at* www.krislindsey.com.

## Real Wealth

### *Ethan Ruoff*

Once there was a very rich man named Ace. When he was born, his family bought him a car seat made of pure gold. On his first birthday, his mom gave him a cell phone. On his second birthday, his dad bought him a brand new car, for when he was older. Everything was handed to Ace on a golden platter. When he entered school, even his teachers were paid to give him no homework.

One day, when he was six years old, he was invited to a birthday party at the park. The generous birthday boy handed out the pizza, keeping the smallest piece for himself. Before they began to eat, he closed his eyes and began praying to Jesus.

Ace asked his father what they were doing, and his father asked the boy to stop praying.

The birthday boy said, "No."

Ace's father pulled out three thousand dollars and again asked the boy to stop praying.

Before his parents could respond, the kid said, "Jesus has given me eternal wealth, and that is more than the wealth of the world."

After a long silence, Ace's father grabbed him and made him leave the party.

When Ace turned eight, his parents decided to let him try school. On his first day of school, he noticed that not everyone had cool cars and golden shoes.

A couple months later, he compared his grades with a girl name Penny, who got her name based on how much money her parents had when she was born. Ace was happy to see that he had an *F* and she had an *A*. "My letter is farther in the alphabet!"

Penny replied, "Actually, *F* is for fail and *A* is for awesome, though I don't want to brag."

Ace wondered, *How could someone so poor get better grades than someone so rich?*

The next day he asked Penny, "What is your secret for getting good grades?"

She replied, "I just trust Jesus and let Him do the rest."

Confused about Jesus, he asked, "Who is Jesus?"

"The Savior of the world."

"What did He do?"

"He died for us."

"But wha—"

"You can find this all in the Bible." Penny handed Ace a Bible.

He took it happily. The next day Ace's father kept him home from school and burned the Bible. Ace was very sad.

A couple years later, when he was in high school, he met Penny again. She invited him to a Christian youth group.

He gladly joined. When he was there, he learned about giving to the needy. He pulled out his wallet and dropped it in the offering bucket. Then and there, he gave his life to Christ. When he got home, he told his father what had happened. His father just sighed and told him to leave.

Over the next couple of years, Ace found the most happiness of his life. He got straight $A$'s, bought a house, and eventually married Penny. Sadly, even though he kept telling his parents about Jesus, they kept rejecting Him.

His father died soon afterwards.

When Ace went to visit his mother, his father's journal was open on the table. Ace read the last entry in the journal: *I have done some research on Christianity, and have decided to follow my son's religion.*

*Ethan Ruoff is a middle school student who attends a Christian school in Northern California and loves God greatly. He loves to have fun and has a great imagination. He used that imagination and started writing when he was eleven.*

# GOD'S CUP OF JOY

## *Sharon Ludden*

The downturn of the economy loomed long and wide, and with the fury of a ruthless intruder it invaded our home. Feeling like a weak-kneed hostage, I questioned how could I muster the emotional fortitude to face this assault.

My husband, Tim, had lost his sales position in the construction trade, and like so many others, we grew concerned and wrestled with how to stave off losses. Thoughts of worst-case scenarios haunted me and thwarted any hint of optimism.

Tim has always done a better job handling the ebb and flow of life. He expresses legitimate concern but seldom falls prey to fear and certainly never hopelessness. He's quick to proclaim that God will show Himself faithful in ways we do not yet understand.

I looked critically at ways to conserve household expenses. We live rather modestly anyway, but still we needed to adjust our life style. What could we give up? Going out to dinner became a rare and treasured extravagance. But what was *I* willing to relinquish?

As an ardent coffee consumer, contemplating the morning's first aromatic sip excites me! I look forward to starting each day with a steaming hot cup of joe and feel cheated and edgy if anything stands between us.

Oh Lord, no! Please don't ask me to give up my coffee! Take the cheddar cheese, the chocolate, the potato chips, my shoe fetish, but not my precious coffee!

Panic soon gave way to reason and curiosity. I performed a few simple calculations and figured out I spent $30 a month on coffee in the cafeteria at work—a resounding $360 a year. Now this grabbed my attention!

While not keen on surrendering my morning ritual, good sense prevailed. I could substitute cafeteria java for a more affordable option. A coffee-loving colleague and I agreed to split the expenses of brewing our favorite blends in a Mr. Coffee maker in the back office. This new twist took on special meaning because it was shared with a friend.

For nearly a decade, squirreling away a modest kitty had become a worthwhile and gratifying life change. And more importantly, God had reminded me repeatedly that He will never leave us nor forsake us, and that His ways are indeed above our ways.

During this season, I received a couple pay raises and a promotion, and my husband landed another job. Even so, God wasn't finished. An unanticipated bonus awaited me in the foyer outside my office.

Whoosh! The aroma of brewed coffee assailed my nostrils. I breathed deeply, thinking my senses betrayed me. But no—

like a warm soothing sauna, the intoxicating fragrance filled my lungs with satisfying pleasure. My heart leapt with joy! Invisible whiffs of wonder beckoned me to follow.

Staff and students passing in the hallway gleefully chatted about a new coffee cafe on the second floor. Needing to see for myself, I hopped into the elevator for a potential joyful ride.

A shiny stainless steel kiosk stationed in the southeast corner displayed signage announcing the "Mean Mugs Café—Coffee with Attitude!" *Swish, slurp, cha ching!* Sounds of success and satisfied customers electrified the air. But now I faced a downright dilemma. Would I stay true to growing the coffee cache, or would I retire Mr. Coffee?

Hmmm. Factoring inflation, the price of a cup of coffee had risen 10% over the past decade. I certainly didn't want to sabotage my savings plan; however, our finances had improved. But could I justify $1.80 per day? *Lord, if it matters, show me what would please You.*

Deciding a taste test was in order, I purchased my first cup of Brazilian brew. I introduced myself to Jillian, the owner, and welcomed her to Sierra College. Surprisingly, I hardly noticed that I'd turned over $2.00. It seemed an equitable exchange. Besides this was only an experiment.

My research lasted one week but proved inconclusive. I hadn't determined whether it would be more prudent to continue my savings practice or treat myself to an exceptional cup of coffee each morning. *Lord, I'm fine either way, but which choice would honor You more?*

During my fact-finding visits to Mean Mugs, I learned that Jillian had an eighteen-year banking background. She'd coached numerous entrepreneurs how to start their businesses and decided it was time to take her own professional advice. I admired her enterprising moxie and speculated that according to the line of new and repeat customers her venture would thrive.

Each day it seemed that Jillian added something new to the cafe: more pastries, bananas, cereal, festive signage, even expanded the footprint by adding another station. One day she said business was so brisk she needed to hire part-time employees—the next day a new friendly face appeared at the cash register. Watching her business take off delighted me. My thoughts brightened as clarity exquisitely established my heart.

God impressed me to invest in Jillian. That it was time to shift my focus from protecting my personal assets to supporting someone else's. What freedom!

Each morning as I approach Mean Mugs Cafe, I revel in a fresh perspective—one that extends far beyond me and my needs. I delight in God and His handiwork, as I drink up a cup of joy.

❧

*Do nothing out of selfish ambition or vain conceit. Rather, in humility value others above yourselves, not looking to your own interests but each of you to the interests of the others.* (Philippians 2:2–4)

*Sharon previously served as treasurer of the Sacramento Christian Writers for twelve years. Sharon's poems and stories are published in the **Inspire Trust** and **Inspire Faith** anthologies. Her personal stories exemplify how God has impacted and transformed her life.*

# THE ROAD TO JOY
## *Janet Ann Collins*

Long, long the road, and we have just begun.

Weary the heart that must go on.

Trust 'til we find,

When wand'ring days are done,

The same hand has led us that guides the moon and sun.


Evil around, and darkness where we are,

Far from us seems the nearest star.

Onward through death

Still leads the Risen One.

Wounded the hand of Christ, the Living Son.

JANET ANN COLLINS

Homeward at last now bends the pilgrim way.

Wondrous the joy for us He won.

His is the hand

That led us day by day.

See how His glory outshines the moon and sun!

*Janet Ann Collins is a grandmother, a retired teacher, and was a foster mother to kids with Special Needs. Her work has been published in many newspapers, periodicals, and anthologies, and she is the author of five books for children. Janet's website is* www.janetanncollins.com.

# ENCOUNTER ON HIGHWAY 50

## *Susan McCrea*

Deep in conversation, my husband, Martin, and I drove east through the thick, rush hour traffic on Highway 50 out of Sacramento. *Crash!* Our car propelled into the back of a pickup truck in front of us. Its license plate was the last thing I saw.

I felt dazed and strangely warm as I sat in the passenger seat. I could not move. I could see nothing. I only heard the door slam as my husband left the car. There were high-pitched voices in the distance.

*God, I am seven months pregnant. How can this be happening to me?*

Our first visit to a gynecologist that November 21, 1974 afternoon had been traumatic. To save money we had postponed getting medical assistance until late in the pregnancy. Hadn't I already had two healthy pregnancies?

"It's a package deal," the receptionist told us. "It doesn't matter what month you begin. It's the same price whenever you start treatment."

Before the appointment, I sat in the reception area next to a young woman waiting for an abortion consultation. The atmosphere of death and depression in the room clouded my happiness over the new life within me.

Martin and I discussed these disturbing events during our drive home. "How are we going to afford that large bill?" I asked. Our $400 a month income left little room for extra expenses after we paid a $200 rent.

The accident ended our stressful conversation. As I sat alone in the car, the warmth I felt in my body troubled me. *Am I bleeding to death?*

A man and a woman came to my car window. "You are going to be all right. We are medical people. An ambulance is coming soon."

*Are they trying to humor me? Am I dying?*

After they left, I cried out loud. "Jesus!" A year before I had surrendered my life to Him after a long struggle and disappointing courtship with New Age teachings. This was the first test of my new-found faith. *Will He come though?*

I could see! An instant after my desperate prayer, I felt wonderful. He filled me with His Spirit. I could hardly contain my joy.

The ambulance came. They lifted me out of our car and placed me on a stretcher inside the back of their van. A young man sat next to me as we wound our way to the nearest hospital. Martin, I was told, followed behind the ambulance in the car of the woman, who had spoken to me.

I asked the ambulance attendant. "Do you know, Jesus? He is real. He gave me back my sight when I called on Him. I feel great."

The young man stared at me as I shared my encounter with Jesus. I think he wondered if I was in my right mind. He did not know how sane I was. I could not contain my joy over Jesus' response to me.

We arrived at Sutter Memorial Hospital's Emergency Room. The first doctor I saw didn't believe me when I told him that I could not move my arms. He wanted me to remove my blouse. Reluctantly he cut off my lovely flower print shirt.

A kind X-ray technician then whisked me off for pictures of my elbows. I told him about the rudeness of the emergency doctor. He encouraged me. "You don't have to stay with him. They will give you a specialty doctor as soon as it's discovered what's wrong with you."

When I returned from the X-rays, Martin had arrived at the emergency room. The nurse who had spoken to me at the accident accompanied him. The other Good Samaritan had been one of the few people at the time to have an emergency phone in his car. I heard later that he had phoned for the ambulance but left the crash scene after it arrived.

The emergency doctor returned to the examination room. "You have two broken elbows," he said. He never apologized for his bad attitude, even after the X-rays showed my fractures. "You came very close to having a concussion."

Martin told me my head cracked the windshield. I had had no seatbelt. My arms had protected my baby.

"You need to be admitted to the hospital and be watched that you don't have a premature delivery. Do you have an orthopedic doctor you would like us to contact?"

We had no idea of a doctor to tell him to call.

The nurse, our angel of mercy, asked Martin. "Do you want me to give you a recommendation?"

"Yes," Martin said.

She gave us the name of a doctor she knew. We thanked her.

I stayed in the gynecology section of the hospital for seven days. My precious child didn't come early as they had feared. My head hurt. Large casts covered both of my immobile arms. I could only move my fingers. I often used them to turn the pages of my comforting, pocket New Testament. Even though I was helpless and dependent, I remained joyful most of the time during my stay. Jesus had met me. I had discovered He is real!

My baby, Rosemary, arrived on February 17, 1975—at the same hospital but with a different gynecologist. My casts had been removed, and my arms had healed enough so that I could just lift my beautiful seven pound, three ounce baby—not an ounce more. A week before her arrival, I could not even carry that much weight. On the day of her birth, when I needed to, I could hold her in my arms.

I look back on that encounter with Jesus on Highway 50 as a pivotal one. It confirmed my faith in Jesus. Even though it was a challenging circumstance, He met my every need through others—the man who called the ambulance, the nurse who provided the name of the bone doctor, both poised nearby on the freeway ready to serve, and the X-ray technician who calmed my fears. Jesus Himself helped me by restoring my eyesight and filling me with His Spirit. My baby not only survived but flourished with a timely birth. In every detail, we were loved and care for. This affirmed my confidence that, even in trials, the Lord would help me.

I follow a living, responsive God. My joy overflows.

*Susan McCrea is a writer and pastor/teacher, who lives in Fair Oaks, California, with her husband, Martin, of forty-five years. She especially enjoys visits from their six children and fourteen grandchildren. At thirty-eight, she discovered she was an adoptee. Her exciting search-and-reunion story should be published soon. To learn more about her story, contact Susan at* www.susanmccrea.com.

# A BITE TO EAT WITH GRANDMA

## *Elaine Faber*

Certain sights and sounds bring back memories that make me smile. An old train…a Dime Store magazine ad…a black lunch pail…

I grew up in Sebastopol—the last Northern California town before entering Oregon—during the time when the railroad train would hold up Main Street traffic several times a day. Passenger service on this line ceased in the 1930s, but regular freight trains continued down Main Street into the late 1970s, long after I graduated from high school.

Sebastopol got its name in 1854 in the newly formed town after a lively fistfight, which was likened to the long British siege of the then-Russian seaport of Svastopol (now part of Ukraine) during the Crimean War.

Because Sebastopol had only one main street, shopping opportunities were limited. When we needed anything beyond the simplest purchase, Mama and Grandma and I would *go to town*, which meant driving to Santa Rosa, seven miles away.

It's funny how our ideas of driving and distance have changed over the years. What used to take a half hour to travel the seven mile distance over bumpy country roads at 30 miles an hour in a stick-shift Buick, now takes seven minutes flat on a blazing freeway in our air-conditioned hybrid Lexus.

*Going to town* with Mama and Grandma was an all-day event. We only went to Santa Rosa to shop for school clothes or Christmas presents or Easter outfits. We would park at the Sears store and walk to Penney's, Kress' Five and Dime, and other specialty shops, often a block or two apart. Shopping malls were still a thing of the future, so we walked, carrying our purchases from store to store. That's probably why they took me shopping with them, to help carry packages.

Finding a dress for Grandma took the greater part of the morning. It required going from shop to shop as she tried on numerous dresses until she found one she liked, at a price she was "willing to give."

One of my favorite memories was going to the Ladies Ready-to-Wear Department in the Penney's Store. They used a *modern* pneumatic tube system for collecting money. Salesladies rang up the merchandise at cash registers strategically placed throughout the store. Not much waiting in line in those days, as the salesladies were numerous and eager to serve. When a purchase was made, she wrote up the sale in duplicate (with carbon paper) in a sales book and placed the sales ticket and our money into a pneumatic tube system, snapped the container, placed it in the tube system and pushed the button.

The container was sucked through the clear plastic tube system, circled the ceiling, ending on the second floor in a locked office where a cashier overlooked the merchandise floor. Each cash register had a separate pneumatic tube container. From where we waited for change, we could see the cashier take the money from the container, place our change and a receipt back into the tube and send it whooshing back through the tube system.

Our tube made its way back across the ceiling and plunked into the tray behind our saleslady. She would open the tube and give us our change and the sales receipt. It took about five minutes for the tube to travel to the cash office, be processed, and return to the customer waiting at the counter. While we waited, I enjoyed watching the various plastic tubes coming and going to various cash registers, like railroad cars on a giant overhead track.

One has to wonder whether the system was in place because it was considered state of the art or if Penney's was suspicious of the saleslady handling so much money, or concerned about armed robbers on the sales floor. I don't recall my mother ever questioning the sensibility of this process or complaining about the length of time she waited to receive her change. One waited patiently, because that's just the way it worked.

At noon, Grandma would suggest that we stop at the Kress's fountain for "a bite to eat," which meant hot turkey sandwiches, mashed potatoes and gravy, and apple pie.

After lunch, we continued our shopping spree. Finally, mid-afternoon, exhausted, each of us hauling big shopping bags filled with the day's purchases, we hiked back to the car and drove Grandma home.

Taking Grandma home took us back down Sebastopol's main street where inevitably we would be delayed by the one working stop light in the center of town or the train making its way slowly down Main Street.

Daddy would come home from a hard day's work carrying lumber, climbing ladders and raising rafters all day, and set his black metal lunch pail on the counter. His red checked shirt, tan coveralls and boots were usually covered with sawdust.

Knowing it was my job to empty his lunch pail and wash out his thermos bottle, he always left a bit of dessert or a snack for me. I would open his lunchbox and find the treat. Maybe it was a chocolate cupcake with pink fluffy coconut frosting. When his lunchbox and thermos were clean, I licked the pink fluffy frosting off the cupcake and we would share a smile across the kitchen. Then, I would show him the new dress or shoes we had bought that day.

Mama would tell him to "get those filthy clothes off and clean up for dinner."

How he must have hated the inevitable words that followed, "We went shopping today. We stopped at Kress's for a bite to eat, so we're just having a light supper tonight."

Daddy was a meat and potatoes man, but Mama never cooked dinner on her shopping days. After a hard day at work, Daddy was befuddled as to why Mama getting "a bite to eat" that afternoon translated into a "light supper" for him that night. I don't suppose he ever went to bed hungry, but he didn't get his meat and potatoes on the days Grandma and Mama stopped for a "bite to eat."

Shopping with Grandma and Mama, hauling packages from store to store, watching the pneumatic tube system at Penney's, getting a bite to eat at Kress's, cleaning Daddy's lunch pail and maneuvering our way through the last town with a train running down Main Street—these are cherished memories. These are memories that bring me joy.

*Elaine Faber is a member of Sisters in Crime, Cat Writers Association, and Inspire Christian Writers, where she serves as an editor for the annual Inspire anthology. Elaine has published four novels, most recently a World War II novel entitled* **Mrs. Oddboddy Hometown Patriot**. *Her short stories are in multiple anthologies.* http://www.mindcandymysteries.com

# Joy
## *Ani Avdalyan*

It's a sense that can last for eternity

A feeling that's not your enemy

An impression that stirs inside of you

And it can excite you, too.


It can sometimes make you smile

Almost as big as a mile

You can share it with your best friends

And then it truly won't end.


Family can give you this feeling

It's one that has lots of meaning

Have you guessed what this secret is yet?

It's something that's never a threat.

Now I want you to see

What this means to me

It's God's gift of joy

And it's not a toy.


Joy is the feeling God gives you

It can make all things new

When you feel His joyful love

You know that it came from above.

*Ani attends a Christian school in Northern California. Her life is dedicated to the Savior, Jesus Christ. In Ani's free time, she likes to spend time with family and friends. Ani has a passion for writing. She loves to use her imagination to write and edit stories.*

# Joy, On the Other Side

## *Pete Cruz*

"Whatever I do isn't good enough for him!" Natalia wailed to her mother as I stood there open-mouthed. Our daughter's sobbing filled the dining area inside our duplex.

The night before, I had slammed my shoes against Natalia's bedroom wall, fully ruining any chances for the both of us to sleep. I couldn't even remember why I was so enraged.

Her mom arrived in the early morning. She observed with arms folded, trying to comprehend my latest eruption, wary her presence could trigger my quick-release temper.

"I just want to stay at your house now, Mom," Natalia whimpered, her deep, brown eyes pleading. Over ten years of equal custody with me since she was a three-year old now came to a head.

"But, I…" was all I could muster.

"I don't think she can stay here anymore," her mother began. The words seared my core being. A surging tide pushed me toward jagged rocks.

"Don't take my daughter away from me! Please, you can't do this to me!" I'd always been too proud to beg for anything. Until now.

"Maybe when she has some time away from you, we can talk about her coming back."

At the entrance hallway next to the dining area I propped my shoulder against the wall. I sagged like a plant needing water, devastated by the thought of losing my daughter. My forehead pressed upon the cool paint of the wall. Anguished tears flooded to the floor so voluminous it resembled a leaking garden faucet. Tears disappeared into the carpet. Some drops rebounded a tiny splash before settling into a damp puddle.

I failed my daughter. I failed myself. Wrenching sorrow overwhelmed me.

"I can't do this, God. I can't escape my past," I breathed in whisper. "I've tried so hard…"

As a youth I promised myself my child wouldn't be raised with the same physical and mental abuse I endured at the hands of my father. My own father used to tell me directly I wasn't good enough. He'd add, "You'll never amount to anything."

Though I never raised a hand to Natalia, I hadn't provided a secure or nurturing environment. I rarely extended a protective arm around her or a daddy's shoulder to cry on. At times I offered encouragement, but not consistently. Terms of endearment were unnatural attempts. I believed her upbringing different than mine, but now sober truth set in.

Natalia experienced a sullen and withdrawn father, a caregiver struggling with depression, unable to control his anger. It shocked me when she declared anything she did wasn't good enough. Our way of life existed because it was the only one I knew. Despite all my love for my daughter, despite all my will for a different outcome, I failed us. Miserably. I admitted to myself, *I placed the eggshells on the floor she stepped upon.*

☙

At lunchtime I sat on the usual park bench across from my job. Sunshine and a soft breeze did nothing to calm my inner storm. Even though it was my week to have Natalia, she stayed at her mom's. I wrestled with the idea it might be better for my daughter to live away from me.

My sterile existence mirrored the glass-windowed walls of the surrounding office buildings. For the last year, I'd gone to psychotherapy twice a week. One counselor treated me for clinical depression, while another focused on PTSD. Neither helped much.

I coped with chronic pain which prevented me from engaging in the activities I most enjoyed. At over fifty years in age, mine was a lifetime of struggle. My future didn't look any better.

"This isn't going to end well," I lamented to God.

A still, small voice welled up within the roiling tumult of my deliberations. *You're going to be all right.* Warmth descended, unlike that of the downtown Sacramento spring day. I peered over my shoulder to be certain no one stood by who spoke assurance. No one was there. A small tear escaped the corner of my eye, running down the side of my face.

I uttered an audible, "Thank You."

In the weeks following, I sought the Lord at a church downtown. After two services, my lifelong depression was gone as if it never before existed. I looked around, dumbfounded, as if searching for misplaced keys, but it was nowhere to be found. I still perceived the floor of despair, but the trap-door which often sent me spiraling far below was now sealed.

☙

Natalia and I regularly attended Harvest Church in Elk Grove, beginning her junior year in high school. I became a member of Honor Bound, the church's men's group. I was initially drawn to these men by the manner in which they treated my daughter. Natalia had grown into a beautiful young woman. Males of all ages often stared at her with lustful eyes. I'd often restrained my revulsion. But with the men at Harvest Church, I saw genuine courtesy. After service the men greeted us warmly and on occasion one would say, "You know, he brags on you," referring to the meetings where I'd become a raw and transparent seeker. I fully pressed near to the Lord, craving an alternative trajectory for me and my family.

The men showed me what a servant of the Lord looks like. They impressed upon me that a father is the priest of his home and it is our duty to bring our family to the Lord.

I couldn't tell what affect my pursuit of God had on my daughter. I didn't know until the end of her high school career, when she applied for college.

~

My daughter's first choice for college was a University of California school, but her combination of GPA and SAT or ACT scores didn't meet admissions requirements. She resolved to attend a junior college to bolster her grades and then apply to a UC later. One school, Biola University, continued to send her inquiry emails. She guessed she must've put her contact information down at a school college fair. Like her, I'd never heard of Biola and didn't know what it meant to attend a Christian university. I thought it clever Biola shortened its name from The Bible Institute of Los Angeles when it moved to Orange County.

"I told my counselor at school, Mrs. Nguyen, that Biola called. I asked her if I should call back. She said I should. Well, I called them and they want me to apply," Natalia remarked as part of her day's events.

"Well, that's good. We'll see what happens." I didn't think anything would happen. I was already used to the idea she would start at the local community college.

Weeks later the familiar creak of the front door sounded as Natalia stepped in after another school day. Her broad smile and bright eyes greeted me.

"Guess what, Dad? An admissions counselor from Biola called me. She said my application was late." Her enthused demeanor suggested I withhold a lecture about waiting until the last minute. "She asked me about the admissions letter I wrote. She said she had a meeting this morning with all the other admissions counselors. She said they began their meeting praying for me. They want me to go there."

A familiar welling up of the Holy Spirit rose inside me as my voice cracked, "God doesn't care about deadlines." I wondered, *what school prays for you? What's in the admissions letter which made them reconsider the late deadline?*

My daughter shared her admissions essay with me. Here, in part, is the last paragraph:

> My father ended up being the biggest miracle in my life. I used to dread the days I would have to spend with him due to his angry and depressed state. Yet, if you were to see him now, he no longer possesses the eyes of hate, or wears the mask of anger. Instead, all that is left is the love he holds for God and for me... Seeing his transformation gives me hope for my own miracles. Though there has not been any grandiose event that has magically cured all my problems, God still transformed my life. The Lord blessed us and His grace is amazing. With His subtle and gentle influences within me and Dad, I know the changes are permanent. Through it all my own father, who I used to hate, brought me to the Father. Now I want to be with the Lord all the time... I believe the Lord has guided me to a path of righteousness, a path which begins with this first step in applying for admission to Biola University.

Sometimes when we go about making plans according to how we see our lives, the Lord shows us He has something bigger and better for us than what we initially conceive. Natalia had already signed up for classes at the local junior college when Biola University called. She later discovered her ACT scores were indeed high enough to attend a UC school, but by then it was too late to apply. She speculated the Lord must've helped her to read it wrong.

The redemptive power of Christ delivered us both to joy, on the other side.

*Pete Cruz is Natalia's father. She's a senior at Biola University and last year spent a semester abroad in Ecuador. Her major is Elementary Education. Natalia holds a 3.7 GPA, and was named to the Dean's List her sophomore and junior years. Pete is overjoyed and still brags on her.*

## WRITER'S JOY
### *Michelle Janene*

A blank page on the screen,

Plots forming in my head.

Fingers dancing over the keyboard,

Clicking and clacking,

Creating a music all their own.

Letter by letter,

Word by word,

Sentence by sentence,

Chapter by chapter.

Characters take form,

Plot takes shape.

Page after page,

Filled from imagination,

And sprinkled with truth.

I am there in between the words,

Hiding in form,

But baring my soul.

Smile plastered to my face,

Merriment dancing in my spirit.

One more paragraph,

One more sentence,

One more word,

It is finished.

Re-read,

Revise,

Edit,

Publish.

Begin again.

A blank page on the screen,

Plots forming in my head.

❧

*Michelle Janene lives in Northern California, though most days she blissfully exists in the medieval creations of her mind. She is a devoted teacher, a dysfunctional housekeeper, and a dedicated writer. Michelle published **Mission: Mistaken Identity** in 2015 and has both contributed to and helped to edit the Inspire Anthologies.* www.TurretWriting.com

# When There's Hope, There's Joy

## *Julie Blackman*

Ruth watched as Dawn tilted her head, looked her up and down, focused on her shoes for a few seconds, then nodded.

*I hope she approves.*

"Good, you're dressed appropriately and wearing comfortable shoes. You'd be surprised how some people show up. I wonder if they're really here to serve or to be seen." They both laughed and walked towards the dining hall. "You'll be on your feet for a while monitoring the tables until everyone is served."

A loud bell rang signaling the commencement of lunch. Dawn, the food bank team director, opened up with a quick welcome speech and said a prayer of blessing over the food.

A roar of chatter erupted after the prayer. Ruth couldn't believe her eyes. The room was filled with men, women, and children of all ages. In addition to food, the shelter provided clothing, showering privileges, hygiene supplies, and a limited number of cots for those who didn't have anywhere to sleep for the night. Women with children were given precedence for the sleeping cots.

"Wow. Is it typically like this?" Ruth asked another volunteer standing nearby.

"This must be your first time. Yep. It doesn't matter what day of the week it is. But weekends are the busiest. I'm just happy that I get to be a part of this."

"I agree."

"Once you've got your set of tables served, keep an eye out to see if anyone wants seconds and make sure everyone gets something to drink. Start up a conversation if you can. It gives them a sense of belonging—at least I think so anyway. I'm on a first name basis with some."

"Thanks for the tips."

After distributing all of the trays of food to her tables, Ruth walked around and served cups of lemonade. She scanned her area to check tables and her eye caught a middle-aged woman sitting *alone* at the end of a table in the back corner. She didn't look like the others, but had a presence about her. Ruth walked over.

"Hi, my name is Ruth, do you mind if I join you and rest my feet a while?"

"Not at all. Thank you so much for serving me today, Ruth. I'm Diana."

"If you don't mind me asking, how long have you been on the streets?"

"Oh it's been about two months now. Although I'm not really on the streets, I live in my car." Diana continued to describe her life. She had a spending problem which resulted in mass credit card debt. Then she lost her job, her apartment, and was now forced to live in her car. About a week ago, it broke down and she tried to find a nearby job to save money for repairs, but without success.

Ruth studied her disposition as she described her situation. Not one ounce of sorrow showed on this woman's face. *How could she be so content?* Diana's eyes sparkled when she spoke and throughout the entire conversation, she smiled.

"I should have been more responsible. Now I'm learning the lesson the hard way."

"You're handling your situation extremely well. How?"

"Trust me, I wasn't always like this. In the beginning, I cried every day. It got to the point that I'd weep throughout mealtime. Poor Dawn, one evening, she begged me to talk to the onsite chaplain, and I did."

Ruth sat back in her chair and listened as the woman shared how the minister had shared with her the love of God and the gift of salvation.

"I fought listening to what he was saying for days. Then it occurred to me, *Jesus is the only one Who can help me.* The rest is history. I see that quizzical look on your face. Ruth, it's all about timing. Things get done on His time not ours. But, I'm confident that something will work out soon. Don't count me out, young lady." She laughed out loud and winked.

"I admire you a lot. You're so upbeat about being homeless." Ruth motioned to Diana to keep eating.

Ruth could overhear other conversations going on. The men grumbled about the lack of money collected for the day, while the women complained about the cold weather. They feared that their children would get sick. Ruth shook her head as tears filled her eyes.

"Oh dear. I hope you're not feeling sorry for me."

"It's not that I'm pitying any of you, I'm just saddened that's all."

"It's a temporary setback, but a teachable moment for me to get my life back on track. I'll be alright."

Ruth couldn't fathom the optimism nor this woman's confidence.

"How can you say that? I hope things change for you, but let's face it, you could be on the streets for a little longer." *Uh oh, way to go Ruth.* To her astonishment, Diana didn't react to the comment at all.

"Because God has heard my prayer—I just know it. Dawn is working to help me get set up with another agency for a place to stay and a contact to help me find a job. Dear, when you have faith in God, He'll give you a joy that's greater than your current situation. I'll never forget the scripture Dawn shared with me when I showed up here two months ago. 'May the God of hope fill you with all joy and peace as you trust in Him, so that you may overflow with hope by the power of the Holy Spirit, Romans 15 verse 13.'"

Diana's eyes sparkled when she recited the scripture.

"This has kept me going over the past couple of months, dear. No use in worrying about the *now*, especially if you're doing all you can. You've gotta focus on the future."

"Diana, Diana!"

They both looked up to see Dawn running towards them waving her hands in the air.

"Hey Dawn, you must have good news for me."

"You know it. I just got an email from one of our partner shelter locations. They have a room and a job-opportunity connection for you. We can get a ride for you right after lunch. Stop by the front desk, I left the information up there for you. Another success story."

"God bless you, Dawn, thank you." Diana turned to Ruth. "Praise God. See, I told you. Don't give up hope. Just trust God and He'll give you the strength to carry on, joy in your heart, and a song on your lips."

"What song did you get?"

"A hymn, *God Will Take Care of You*, written by Civilla D. Martin. Look it up."

"You're truly an inspiration to me, Diana. I'm honored to meet you and glad I came here tonight. Thank you."

"No, my dear, thank you!"

## JULIE BLACKMAN

Julie Blackman writes fiction short stories and nonfiction inspirational pieces. Her desire is to be a writing instrument for the Lord. She enjoys encouraging others whenever possible, and sees her writings as one more avenue to do so. Her works have been published in **Inspire Victory**, **Inspire Promise**, and **Inspire Forgiveness**.

# REMINDING MY HEART TO FLY

## *Susan Sage*

I watched as my students made their way outside. As other classes dismissed, children surged to the playground for recess. One boy burst through his classroom door, threw his arms out from his sides like an airplane and ran around the hardtop. Some children glanced at him as he ran by. A few laughed. Most ignored him, while the eyes of others followed with raised eyebrows.

The little boy smiled as his chin tipped up and his eyes searched the patches of white overhead. He slowed as smaller children crossed his route, yet he didn't stop.

Even the older boys who called out didn't deter him. "You haven't left the ground yet," one scowled as he yelled.

"Run faster, maybe you'll take off," another called after him.

Still, nothing stole the boy's purpose or wiped the smile from his face. Wind blew his dark hair as he jumped across a ball and continued running.

A single tear spilled down my face, as I observed from the window of my classroom. I watched for a moment longer before turning back to stacks of papers waiting for correction.

The desire to fly like the little boy, not leaving the ground yet with my heart so filled with possibilities, stirred deep inside like butterfly wings caressing my stomach. Memories bombarded my mind like a torrent. I fought to focus, yet still those recollections came.

Always the rule follower, I played the same lines in my mind. *Be what others want. Act right. Sit up straight. Don't talk when it's not your turn. Keep your thoughts to yourself; no one wants to hear them. Fold your hands in your lap. Look right, act right, be right.*

When with one group, be who they think you should be. But, in the next group, change like a chameleon. Make others happy so they'll like you. Give treats to buy approval. By all means, don't be yourself...that's dangerous. *Would those voices ever stop?*

Fighting to concentrate on the papers in front of me, my eyes drifted back to the window.

I wanted to be out there, running freely, breathing deeply, no cares to slow me down. Finally, the ringing of the school bell saved me.

I stood, forcing one step and then another, trudging down the cream-textured hall to retrieve my students. Thoughts jumbled through my mind as I struggled to focus. *Just make it down the hallway and out the door. My students will distract me. How can I rise above the multiple voices in my head and stay true to the only important Voice?*

Phrases of a verse quieted the plethora of thoughts. *The Lord is mighty to save. He delights in me. He quiets me with His love and rejoices over me with singing.* (Zephaniah 3:17)

Eyes damp with tears, I drew in a ragged breath. *God delights, loves, and sings over me.* As my heart filled with hope, joy broke through. More memories pushed their way to the surface.

Instantly, I stepped back, over two decades ago.

❧

I saw myself standing on the banks of Lake Ontario. The sun shone on the water like light off a diamond. My shoulders shook, my gut wrenched, my head pounded. I bent down, picked up five stones, and rubbed them in my hands.

*Why would You want me? I'm broken. I can't do anything right. I don't meet anyone's expectations, not even my own. I'm not pretty. I'm not skinny. Why do You care?*

I jostled the textured stones and wiped my shirtsleeve across my eyes.

*You want me? You really want me, Lord? Then You're going to have to take me the way I am. I'm not perfect, but I guess You already know that. Here I am. I don't know why You'd want me. I don't know what I can give You. But, if You want me, then take over and I'll do whatever You want.*

I drew my arm back and threw those stones into Lake Ontario with a pitcher's arm. The self-doubt and loathing that I'd carried every day of my twenty-one years seemed to sprout wings and soared with the stones. Like a bag of boulders, the weight lifted from my shoulders. I didn't dare move for fear of the lightness leaving. The stones dropped as one, sending ripples back to shore. Waves lapped against the sand and rocks.

*What is this? Peace...hope...joy?*

"You heard me," I whispered.

The lake stilled and the breeze settled. All motion seemed to stop. I raised my chin, looking up into fluffs of white clouds hovering over the bluest water.

*Okay, let's go. Whatever, wherever. If You can do what You just did, I can't wait to see what's next.*

ॐ

As suddenly as the memory came, it vanished. The muscles around my eyes tightened as I rubbed my fingers across them. These many years later, here I stood in a similar moment of frustration and weight pulling me down. Words from the same verse played through my mind again. I had forgotten the hope and joy of the day at Lake Ontario. I'd told Him if He wanted me, I would be His—flaws included.

So, what happened? Why did I let everything drag me back to how I was before that victorious day?

I had allowed pressure and the expectations of others to darken the time on the shore. I permitted it.

Realization settled on me like a hummingbird suspended over a bush. I looked out to the playground as the children ran to line up after recess. The little dark-haired boy brought up the rear of his line with his face still lifted toward the clouds.

I walked the lighted hallway to bring my class back into our room. Once again, I sensed the resolve of the previous turning point. I blinked, pulled my shoulders back, straightened up to my full five-foot two-inch height, as renewed focus rooted itself.

"Never again, Lord. Never again. Help me not to forget again."

One of my students turned and looked at me. "What'ja say, Mrs. Sage?"

I reached my arm around her shoulder. "I was just talking to God." With each step, God's joy began taking back its ground and the wings in my heart opened.

*Susan Sage loves the adventure of writing. She writes Bible studies, devotionals, poems, dabbles in fiction, and is currently in re-writes for her first non-fiction book. Susan also speaks to women's groups whether teas, retreats, luncheons or wherever God gives the opportunity. Her passion is encouraging women in their walk with God, no matter where His sovereign plan takes them. Currently, she is focusing that encouragement to those who live with chronic illness and pain. You can find her at* susansage.com, @SusanMSage, *on Facebook, Google+, and Pinterest where she posts her weekly blog.*

# Sunday Morning Joy

## *Ruth Morse*

My joy in teaching Sunday School started last summer. I told my husband I missed my interactions with the children in the libraries where I had worked. Recently retired, I wanted to spend some volunteer time with young ones but hadn't found my niche.

While meeting with someone from my small church, she just happened to say they were looking for a Sunday school teacher. My husband gave me a knowing glance. The next thing I knew, my background check was completed, and I was spending Sunday mornings with a wide range of children under the age of twelve. The church congregation had dwindled and was struggling. There was even a period of time with no childcare or Sunday school at all because of low attendance.

When I started teaching, we had four to six children a week. Currently, on average, we have eight to twelve children and are growing. With two paid daycare helpers who assist with the preschoolers, young bodies flow back and forth between the nursery and Sunday school rooms.

We follow a curriculum, but for me the most important part is when the children and I read and discuss the Scriptures together. One Sunday, the passage was from Mark:

*While Jesus was having dinner at Levi's house, many tax collectors and sinners were eating with him and his disciples, for there were many who followed him.* (Mark 2:15)

"I have a friend in my class named Levi," Abigail*, a pupil in my class, said.

"Yes, do you remember when we studied Genesis and the twelve tribes of Israel? Levi was one of the twelve sons of Jacob and a brother to Joseph. Therefore, it is a person's name." I liked it when my children tracked and interacted with the Scripture. It kept me on my toes.

*These are the names of the sons of Israel (Jacob and his descendants) who went to Egypt: ... The sons of Levi: Gershon, Kohath and Merari.* (Genesis 46:8, 11)

We continued our Bible study from Mark. Abigail made another connection. "My brother Benjamin wears Levi's."

"Yes, these days, jeans are called Levi's because the head of the company many years ago was named Levi Strauss." Inwardly, I wondered if he was Jewish. I made a note to look it up at home after church. And, sure enough, he was a German Jewish immigrant.

I told my husband about the questions and comments in Sunday school when I came home. He suggested that now the poor kids would think that one of Jacob's sons made the original Levi's. I hope I was clearer than that, but at least the story made them think.

We retrieve Bibles from the shelves every week and open them to the appropriate passage. I remember when Maria*, a spunky kindergartner, visited for the second time. We sat around a table with our Bibles, and she said, "We read that book last week."

Out of the mouth of a babe! After letting her know that there is more than one story in the Book, I pondered her statement. I found her comment profound. We do read the Book every week, but it is like no other. It is not boring to repeat passages, because they always speak to us in different ways. What she meant in her naïve comment made me realize just how special the Bible is.

My class is a mix of *churched* and *unchurched* children. This makes for some interesting interactions. Sunday mornings with my Sunday school class often held surprises. This Easter was no exception as I taught about the Resurrection. We had more children than usual.

Michael*, the grandchild of one of our choir members, rarely attends church. After the Easter egg hunt, I read about Jesus appearing to the disciples after the Resurrection. This was when Michael questioned, "Was Jesus a zombie?"

"Not really. Zombies are different than Jesus," I replied. "Jesus was able to have Thomas feel His side and see His wounds from his crucifixion. Zombies aren't that solid. Also, Jesus ate with His friends. Zombies can't eat." In a truly strange twist, the pastor's sermon the very next week was about zombies.

I have puzzled about why teaching gives me such joy. I love seeing the children Sunday mornings. I think it's because I am actively participating in several things that give humans a sense of fulfillment, because we are formed in the image of God. He created us to use our spiritual gifts, witness to others and unselfishly demonstrate His love to the world. For me, these translate into teaching Sunday school. When we do what God has called us to do, we experience true joy.

*There are different kinds of gifts, but the same Spirit distributes them. There are different kinds of service, but the same Lord.* (1 Corinthians 12:4–5)

When I was younger, I thought God would probably have me do something for Him that I loathed. At the top of that list of dreaded tasks was being a physical education teacher. I hated physical education. I was wrong. Instead, my delight with children turned out to be a key to my happiness.

Children were and are very important to God and His Son, Jesus. Just look at the passage in Matthew:

*He called a little child to him, and placed the child among them. And he said: "Truly I tell you, unless you change and become like little children, you will never enter the kingdom of heaven. Therefore, whoever takes the lowly position of this child is the greatest in the kingdom of heaven. And whoever welcomes one such child in my name welcomes me.* (Matthew 18:2–5)

Introducing young ones to Christ is an awesome responsibility, but also a learning experience. I never know what the students will come up with, and I love their fresh views on things that I have taken for granted. Bible study information that I have gleaned over the years is put to good use, and I delight in passing it on to the newest generation. That is the church's present and future. It is said that God has no grandchildren and we need to pass on our wisdom to those who will follow after us. How amazing that God made us in His image and when we align with Him, it brings us joy because He is the source.

Teaching Sunday school took me by surprise. I have learned much. Joy comes in the mornings on Sundays.

*Names have been changed.

*Ruth Morse is a recently retired librarian who is fulfilling a lifelong dream of writing about her experiences. Retirement has brought its own set of challenges, including moving to Northern California and learning how to maximize her time and her joy.*

## Come All Ye Saints!
### *Heather D. Blackman*

Come all ye saints and rejoice with me!

Let us exalt His name together,

For He is faithful, holy, and true,

And His mercies endure forever!


Come all ye saints and sing with me!

Let us burst into jubilant song,

For we lift up our voices to glorify God,

And worship Him all the day long!


Come all ye saints and give thanks with me!

Let us praise His wonderful name,

For we are redeemed by the blood of the Lamb,

And thank God we're no longer the same!

Come all ye saints and rejoice with me!

Let us exalt His name together,

For the joy of the Lord is our shield and our strength,

And His mercies endure forever!

*Heather D. Blackman recently rediscovered her passion for writing poetry as an extension of her creative spirit. Her poetry has been published in **Inspire Promise** and **Inspire Forgiveness**. It is Heather's desire that her poems will uplift, encourage, and express the love of our Heavenly Father.*

# A KISS FOR MY FATHER

## *Debbie Jones Warren*

"You're so sweet," Dad murmured and he turned his weary eyes up to me after I kissed him on the cheek. He lay on a hospital gurney awaiting surgery. Worn out from tests and scans after his recent fall, Dad's grayish cheeks were sunken in like a skeleton, and his breathing hardly registered on the monitor hanging above his bed.

Four months earlier, Dad had undergone emergency open-heart surgery. We feared he wouldn't pull through. For thirty days my emotions roller-coastered from highs of elation to my heart crashing flat on the ground. The morning Dad first swallowed solid food again, my feet did a happy dance on the tiled hospital floor. Two days later my chest tightened with fear when Dad had to return to ICU.

But after four long weeks in the hospital, our valiant trouper was finally released to a rehab facility. Joy! I felt it welling up from my toes, through my body, and bursting out the top of my head at the prospect of a new life for him.

Dad diligently did his physical therapy exercises, continued to gain strength, and was soon preparing to transfer back home to live again with Mom, the light of his life. Then the unthinkable happened. Just before Thanksgiving he fell and cracked the back of his head. The emergency room doctor declared he needed to have minor surgery to drain some blood from his skull.

≈

As I waited by his side in the emergency room and watched my once-strong father laboring with each breath, I flashed back to my teen years when I started pulling away from my parents. Emotionally I grew distant from them, and the day came when I no longer welcomed their warm embrace. I turned away from their kisses, and my parents looked so hurt. Fortunately, as I grew older and had children of my own, my close relationship with Mom and Dad returned.

But I still preferred not to kiss them, especially not on the lips. So instead, my father took his cue and began greeting me as he had done in my early years, planting a kiss on the top of my head. That made me grin as it transported me back to carefree days of childhood, and I appreciated his respect of my boundaries as a young woman now.

≈

Drawing my thoughts back to the present, I bent over the gurney and gently kissed Dad again on the cheek. Opening his eyes wide, he smiled up at me. "That's so precious," he exclaimed. I leaned forward and kissed him once more, this time on his lips. That moment is frozen in my memory. Turning his head slowly toward me, his eyes sparkled and his whole face lit up. "That's even *more* precious!" he whispered.

"I love you, Daddy," I replied with a bright smile as I stood up. I felt a butterfly of hope flit through my stomach: forgiveness extended, forgiveness received. Tears moistened my cheeks, yet a warm blanket of peace had settled around my shoulders as the orderly wheeled the gurney through the operating room doors.

The procedure should have been simple, and initially it was. But my dad's heart, worn down from the events of the past weeks, couldn't take any more strain. Perhaps it was the anesthesia that was the final straw. But whatever the reason, just as he started to regain consciousness after the surgery, his heart rate plummeted. It dropped to thirty, then twenty beats per minute. The doctors and nurses did everything they could medically do. But nothing worked. Dad's heart stopped and he was gone.

↵

Sometimes joy comes from the most unexpected sources. And today mine is the ultimate joy: a relationship reconciled before time ran out. Whenever I reflect back on that day, I am filled anew with gratitude that God gave me the opportunity to step into the pre-op room and kiss my father one last time.

*Born in Alameda, Debbie Jones Warren grew up in Nigeria with missionary parents. She took a degree in business from Fresno State and married Chris Warren, a corporate pilot based in Oakland. They have three young adult children, and one daughter-in-law. Writing helps her make sense of the world.*

# God's Joy Comes in the Morning
## *Millie Andres*

Oh listen, Sadness, you have but this day,

To make me feel hopeless and to wallow in this pain.

Oh listen, Sadness, you have been with me for too long,

But you will CEASE to be in me by break of next dawn.

For JOY comes in the morning my God has said to me,

He will wipe away my tears and He will set me free.

For JOY comes in the morning,

Sadness, you will only last for this night,

For I will be rejoicing in the next morning LIGHT!

Oh listen, Sadness, you have ripped everything from me,

You have taken my heart and left it empty.

Oh listen, Sadness, I will not walk lifeless anymore,

For the LORD MY GOD is knocking at my door!

For JOY comes in the morning my God has said to me,

He will wipe away my tears and He will set me free!

For JOY comes in the morning,

Sadness, you will last for this night,

For I will be rejoicing in the next morning LIGHT!

*Millie Andres is a seventeen-year breast cancer survivor, and through her cancer journey to this day, God has been her foundation and source of inspiration. She cares for her ninety-three-year-old mother, who has dementia. Millie is presently a part of Tweeting God's Love with Cheri Douglas.*

# THE START OF THE WARRIOR

## *Emma Cartwright*

"Daisy!" I screamed as my sister was carried off into the dark night by a small group of attacking soldiers. Suddenly I opened my eyes. My heart was pounding.

"It was only a dream. It was only a dream. It was only a—" I stopped short, then I breathed a sigh of relief and stared out my balcony window. The rain pounded on the glass window like a drummer beating on his drum. It had been going nonstop for five days. Wind howled down the chimney. The trees lay broken everywhere. Would the rain ever stop? There was no way for me to practice my archery. I was stuck inside, bored out of my mind. I know princesses aren't supposed to be interested in anything to do with weapons, but I was. Any opportunity I got, I went to my refuge in the forest, where I practiced archery for hours upon hours.

My mother didn't quite approve of me shooting arrows. But it was kind of her fault for naming me Alessia, which literally means warrior, or defender of man.

℘

I plopped down in front of my tutor. I had no chance of going to the forest. I was stuck in class, history to be exact, and I hated history.

Suddenly, my governess rapped my desk to bring me out of my daze. The history of Corona: and the founder, and blah, blah, blah. History was a bore, but my next class, my "Queen in Training" class, where I learned how to be royal properly, was torture. I practiced how to drink tea, make tea, serve tea, and the history of tea, all in twenty minutes. Then I learned which fork, spoon, or knife to use, how to balance books on my head, and a lot that I don't really think is important. What if I failed to be a good daughter, since I couldn't pay attention?

I respected my parents' wishes. My father, King Maxwell, was the kindest man in our whole kingdom. My mother, Queen Susan, was strict, but I knew she meant well. I had a younger sister too. Princess Daisy was the sweetest, most tender girl I knew. The most important person in my life, however, was God, YHWH, I AM, the Lord God Almighty. I could spend hours praying to Him, singing to Him, loving Him. Which is why I at least tried to pay attention in my classes.

Later that night, I fell asleep to the gentle pitter-patter of the rain on the roof of the castle. It was finally letting up. I prayed the nightmares would not return.

The next morning, the sun shone bright in a blue sky with white puffy clouds. I threw on my favorite day dress and my comfiest flats. It was Saturday. No fluffy dresses, no heavy jewelry, no being a princess. I packed a bag with my Bible, a small scroll, a quill, and an inkpot. I grabbed my bow and arrow, snatched a biscuit, and flew out the palace doors. On my horse, Twilight,

I rode deep into the forest to my private archery ring. I shot arrows, hitting the targets one after the other.

A scream tore through the air. A second answered. Were we under attack? I jumped on Twilight and raced back.

When I arrived through the back of the palace, I slid off Twilight and hurriedly tethered her in her stall. Then I crept into the secret tunnel leading to a secret room we used for safety. At the end of the tunnel, I found my family, and the servants and butlers, huddled together. Daisy was crying, so I ran over to her. I wasn't worried. We had food stocked up, should the rebels stay for days.

☙

After six days, I'd had it! I decided it was time to do something. I gathered my thoughts, pulled my scroll and inkpot from my bag, and wrote out my plan. I spent hours writing and rewriting the battle plan. There was no easy way around it. We couldn't attack from inside because they might be waiting for us at the door. But we also couldn't go through the tunnel again, because even if they were not at the end, we would blow our cover if we showed our faces.

Then I realized I had been forgetting something. I needed to consult someone for help. I found the Bible, slipped into a quiet corner, and opened it. The Bible and God are some of the most important things to me, but I hadn't thought about either this past week.

I prayed for wisdom, guidance, and joy. Joy is the thing I needed most. I had been down lately because I hadn't been able to see the fun in the stuff I was doing, and I worried about the future constantly. I needed to put the future in God's hands and let Him do the rest. I knew only then would I receive true joy and peace.

After my devotion, I returned to my work with a new sense of joy. I no longer felt a pang of fear. I felt joy and hope. Now I was able to come up with a good plan. I couldn't get any of our soldiers hurt, so I would have to go alone. No one would suspect a fifteen year old girl—especially a princess—to fight, but I had the best Warrior on my side. I also had this Warrior's many truths hidden in my heart. The Lord would help, so I could overcome any battle thrown my way. Joy flooded my heart knowing God would fight for me.

I grabbed my arrow quiver. "Mom, Dad, I am going out to the battlefield to fight the army. I will be back as soon as it is over."

I allowed my mom ten minutes of bawling on my shoulder, then left when she wasn't looking. I snuck up the flight of stairs leading to the palace foyer, hunched over so I wasn't visible through the windows, and ran to the doors. The two palace guards tried to stop me for my protection, but I squeezed through their strong arms. They ran after me, but I was too quick because I was armor free. I opened the doors, ran outside, and slammed the doors behind me.

I pulled an arrow from my quiver and aimed it at the war leader. I shot a prayer up, and drew my bow. I took a deep breath in and let it out slowly as I concentrated on my arrow, and then released it. It hit the leader and he collapsed to the ground. This sent his soldiers into a frenzy. They all screamed like babies and ran in every direction. I fired three more quick shots, hitting a group of nearby cavalrymen. That caused the ones who were left to retreat. I'd released all doubt and let God take the reins on all the decisions, and He won the battle.

"The siege is over. It is safe to return," I called. My family, the servants and butlers, and the soldiers who had been manning the wall soon started marching towards me like they were in a parade.

My mother ran to me, beaming with pride. Next came Daisy, who handed me a handful of beautiful flowers she had picked from the royal garden on the way. Then came my father, and after a tight squeeze, he said, "I am so happy for you, honey."

"Thanks, Dad."

"Thank you, Alessia. We are so thankful for your courage," said the servants and butlers.

That night, the cooks made my favorite foods: stuffed quail, mashed potatoes, and biscuits and gravy. I ate until I was stuffed. Unfortunately, I had to give a speech.

"Hello fellow acquaintances. I suppose I am supposed to be saying how proud of myself I am, or what I did to accomplish this great feat, but I am not going to. There is only one simple explanation for this victory—and every victory for that matter. God chose the leader to fight at the appointed time. Today, it happened to be me. I am no special archer or warrior. I am simply me, a sinner, who God, by His mercy, saved and used to accomplish His plan. When you listen to His voice, He gives you a sense of true joy, which I can happily say I have received today. What I say to you is, "Do the same thing." If God gives you a crazy idea, take it, and you too will receive true joy."

*Emma Cartwright currently attends a Christian school in California while on leave from missionary work in Costa Rica with her family. In her free time, Emma loves to dance. She also enjoys picking up a good book, and not putting it down until it is finished.*

# JOY IN THE JOURNEY

## *Karen Foster*

My back stiffened against the leather passenger seat of our rental car. I wrinkled my nose. "Smells like diesel fuel in here."

"Yep," our fifteen-year-old son, Jason, chimed in from the back seat. "I smell it too."

My husband, Dan, glanced over his right shoulder at the German map splayed across our son's lap. "How far's the next town?"

"I'm not sure. Mom just handed me the map."

"Sorry about my navigating skills," I said. "It's not easy reading German roads signs. But at least we're heading in the right direction."

Fertile farmland stretched for miles on either side of the rural, two-lane highway. I preferred this less traveled road rather than the fast-paced autobahn. However, my muscles tensed as the fumes grew stronger.

Dan frowned and switched on the blinker. "I need to pull over and check it out." We turned right, onto a gravel road that paralleled the highway. Just in time. Black smoke curled skyward from the seams of the car hood. We threw open the doors and escaped into the fresh air.

While the guys headed to the front of the SUV, I raised the rear hatch and single-handedly yanked three black roll-on suitcases onto the ground. "Thanks for the help."

"*Aww*," Jason said, "the smoke's already gone."

When the engine cooled, my husband opened the hood and stood back. "Karen, turn on the engine."

"Is it safe?"

Jason grinned. "I'll do it."

"No!" I got into the driver's seat and held my breath as I turned the key.

The two of them jumped back. "Turn it off!"

I hurried to my husband, who pointed to a damp, black rubber hose. "That's the fuel line. The hose split and fuel sprayed out of it when you turned on the engine."

Jason kicked the front tire. "Sounds like we rented a lemon."

I sighed and scanned the plump cornfields that encircled us. A few hours earlier, I'd stood at the bedroom window of our bed and breakfast in a town built during medieval times. My heart soared as I watched a rose-colored sun rise over emerald green hills. And my lips praised God for our fairy-tale vacation.

I hadn't expected this speed bump.

Not that a broken car is the end of the world, but there were hurdles. We didn't speak German. Our cell phones didn't work overseas. Even if we could call for assistance, we didn't know our exact location. My heart sank as joy evaporated into the summer sky.

Then God reminded me of a talk I'd been preparing for a women's event. The theme? "Joy in the Journey." A sheepish grin gathered on my face. I raised my arms toward the powder-blue sky. "Lord, I can't wait to see how you're going to rescue us. Help us find joy in this journey."

"This isn't like you," Dan said. "Normally, you'd be wringing your hands."

I smiled. "Let's count our blessings. We ate a hearty breakfast. We have water bottles. The day is young, and we're not in the boondocks. Besides, God's in control. He'll send help. We just…"

A flatbed truck's engine gears shifted and groaned as it approached us. I waved my arms. Hopped up and down. The male driver glanced our way and barreled passed us.

My husband rolled his eyes. "What'd you say about joy in the journey?"

"I'll bet this gravel road leads to those houses," Jason said. "Maybe we could walk there."

We looked in the direction he pointed. A cluster of slanted rooftops peeked over the distant cornfields. I closed my eyes. "Lord, please send someone to loan us a phone so we can call for help."

Fifteen minutes later, a male driver in an eighteen-wheeler truck turned off the highway and stopped two hundred feet from us. "Thank you, Lord." I grabbed the rental car agreement from the glove compartment. "Let's hope he has a cell phone we can borrow."

"I think you should go alone," Dan said. "That way we'll seem like less of a threat."

I raised my eyebrows.

"It's not that far. I'll be watching you."

I squared my shoulders and power walked to the truck despite the butterflies colliding in my stomach. The driver's window was open, but the stocky, middle-aged man didn't get out of his truck. Instead, he unwrapped a foot-long sandwich.

*Silly me for assuming he'd pulled over to help us.*

"Excuse me. Do you speak English?"

He stared down at me and kept chewing.

"Sorry to bother you, but our car broke." I pointed toward our car in case he hadn't noticed the raised hood. "Do you have a cell phone I could use?" I mimicked holding a phone to my ear.

He glanced in his rearview mirror. Frowning, he handed me a sticky flip phone as though I'd asked for cash. My fingers trembled as I looked at the rental agreement and punched in the phone number.

*Ringggg. Ringggg.* "Please pick up the phone," I whispered.

A male voice with a heavy, German accent answered. "Gutten tag."

"Hello. Do you speak English?"

After a long pause, he said, "Ja, how may I help you?"

I explained our situation and nodded when the truck driver tapped his watch.

"Where are you now?"

"*Uh*...good question." I looked at the driver. "Where are we?"

He mumbled something unintelligible.

"Sorry." I blushed and handed him the phone. "Would you mind telling him our location?"

Their conversation lasted sixty seconds. Then he hung up and started his engine. "They're coming."

"Who? Did he say when they'll be here?"

He wiped his mouth with the back of his hand and repeated, "They're coming."

I stepped back and pinched my nose to avoid inhaling the exhaust pipe fumes as the truck lumbered away. I looked up at the sky, shading my eyes from the sun directly overhead. "Consider it all joy when we encounter trials. Right, Lord?"

I fanned myself with the rental agreement and walked back to my husband. "They're coming."

"Who's coming?"

"Roadside assistance." I leaned against the car's warm metal and chuckled. "Then again, a Wiener Schnitzel truck could be coming."

He stared at me as though I was speaking German.

"Look, Mom. Three's the charm."

A woman driving a white Volkswagen pulled up next to us and rolled down her window. She asked a question in German.

I returned her smile. "Do you speak English?"

"Little bit."

My heart swelled twice its size.

Meanwhile, a tall, lanky teenage boy had stepped out of her car. He stood over our engine—the stench of fuel still in the air—and lit a cigarette. Dan gasped and pulled him away from the car.

The next moments were an amusing compilation of pantomime and awkward dialogue. The woman went home and returned with a cell phone. Dan called the rental car agency in Frankfurt and recounted our plight. He then handed the phone to the woman sitting in her car. "He wants to talk to you."

While she spoke in German, Dan updated Jason and me. "I'm staying with our car while the two of you go with her to an Audi repair shop. She'll coordinate between the mechanic and rental car folks to send us a tow truck.

"What happened to the other tow truck?"

"Who knows, but there's a Ford dealer an hour from here. If they can't fix the car today, they'll give us another one."

Jason and I squeezed into the back of the Volkswagen while the teenager sat in the passenger seat. The four of us were mute on the fifteen-minute ride to town, but I kept smiling. *Thank you, Lord, for a stranger's act of kindness in a foreign land.*

When we arrived at the auto shop, Jason headed for a vending machine while I stood in the oil-stained garage like a helpless child. The woman explained the situation to a man in greasy overalls. Phone calls were made. Papers signed. Then another man in a beige jumpsuit gestured toward a yellow tow truck in the parking lot.

"Time to go," I told my son. "We're riding back to Dad in the tow truck."

"Sweet."

I turned to the woman. My eyes watered. How could I express my gratitude and the childlike joy bubbling in me? Did she realize God had used her to answer my prayers? Even if I could speak German, words seemed inadequate.

The woman's blue eyes widened as I spread my arms around her and squeezed tight. I don't know if she sensed my joy. Or saw the skip in my step when I walked away. But I smiled and gave a thumbs up when I climbed into the back of the tow truck. Eager to enjoy the rest of our day.

*Karen's passion is God's Word. Her family is her joy. She has written for devotionals and personal narrative stories for many Christian publications such as the **Upper Room**, and **Bible Advocate's** magazine: Now What? You can read her blog at* KarenFosterMinistry.com. *Karen's married and has three grown children.*

# INDEX OF CONTRIBUTORS

# Index of Contributors

**Inspire Press is a division of**

# INSPIRE CHRISTIAN WRITERS

Inspire Christian Writers provides a network of support, encouragement, education, and spiritual growth for Christian writers. We minister biblical truths with excellence, clarity, and love, to transform lives and the publishing industry. To learn more and/or join, please visit **inspirewriters.com**

**Also available from Inspire Press**
**INSPIRE TRUST, 2012**
**INSPIRE FAITH, 2013**
**FRIENDS OF INSPIRE FAITH, 2013**
**INSPIRED GLIMPSES OF GOD'S PRESENCE, 2013**
**INSPIRE VICTORY, 2014**
**INSPIRE PROMISE, 2014**
**Exit Cyrus, 2014**
**DogSpirations, 2015**
**How to Love God with All Your Heart, 2015**
**INSPIRE FORGIVENESS, 2015**

**Coming Fall 2017 from Inspire Press**

## INSPIRE LOVE

To receive submission guidelines and/or publication information, please email **inspirepress@inspirewriters.com**

CPSIA information can be obtained
at www.ICGtesting.com
Printed in the USA
FSOW02n0028071016
25716FS